EMPOWERING COMMUNITIES

*Creating a Sustainable System of
Community Wealth and Social Change*

RICHARD RAWSON

Empowering Communities: Creating a Sustainable System of Community Wealth and Social Change

Richard Rawson

Published by:
Rawson Internet Marketing
PO Box 2511
Leesburg, VA 20177 USA

ISBN-13: 979-8-9878416-1-7

Never doubt that a small group of thoughtful, committed citizens can change the world; indeed, it's the only thing that ever has.

—Margaret Mead

Contents

INTRODUCTION

What's Going On

Growing up during the 1960s and 1970s instilled in me a passion for social change, an energy that continues to guide my life. The turbulence of this formative period in American history planted the seeds for an enduring commitment to seek out ways to use my privilege and talent to create opportunities for social change. My initial career interests centered on understanding and alleviating behavioral and psychological issues across a wide range of contexts. It was my way of making a difference in the lives of individuals, families, and communities. From this orientation, I began to recognize the profound and sometimes subtle ways in which individuals and communities have been disadvantaged by systemic disparities—the unequal distribution of resources, opportunities, and power between different groups in society.

This inequality is often based on race, gender, class, and other social identities that are linked to historical oppression and discrimination. Systemic disparities can be seen in a variety of areas including education, employment, housing, healthcare access and quality of care, criminal justice system involvement, and wealth accumulation. The privatization of public services has created or worsened social inequalities by making basic services inaccessible or unaffordable for those who need them most. Overall, systemic disparities are rooted in structural inequalities that have been perpetuated over time through policies and practices that favor certain groups while disadvantaging others based on race or other social identities. These disparities continue today despite efforts by many organizations and individuals working towards greater equity across all sectors of society.

Against a backdrop of sweeping social change and turmoil, the '60s and '70s were also characterized by an unwavering spirit of optimism. It was during this time that civil rights, the women's movement, environmental issues, and other progressive movements began to gain traction. As a young person, I was deeply inspired by these efforts, particularly the underlying sense of solidarity and collective action in the pursuit of social justice. The Kennedy, Shriver, and King families were at the forefront of progressive movements in the United States during the 20th century.

The Kennedy agenda included support for civil rights legislation, expansion of Social Security benefits, and increased access to education. They also founded the Peace Corps, which sent volunteers abroad to promote peace and development around the world. Sargent Shriver's War on Poverty created programs such as Head Start to provide educational opportunities for disadvantaged children. He also established Job Corps to help young people gain job skills and find employment. Martin Luther King Jr.'s leadership of the Civil Rights Movement resulted in significant legislative victories for African Americans, including the passage of the Civil Rights Act of 1964 and the Voting Rights Act of 1965.

What is Solidarity and Why is it Important?

It was clear to me then, as it is now, that social change requires a comprehensive effort by various individuals and organizations to create a sustainable system of community wealth and social change. The concept of solidarity is fundamental to this effort. Solidarity seeks to build alliances and networks between people from different backgrounds, cultures, and social identities to create a more just and equitable society. This requires working together to identify and address issues of injustice, oppression, and discrimination as well as creating positive change by advocating for public policies that support the collective well-being of all members of society. Moreover, solidarity is an essential part of building healthy communities by fostering a sense of belonging and compassion for one another. Societies have pulled together in times of crisis—from the World Wars and global pandemics to local natural disasters and personal struggles—it is in these moments of hardship that people realize the potential and power of solidarity.

Margaret Mead, a renowned American cultural anthropologist, declared that the only thing capable of truly changing our world is an assemblage of devoted citizens. She stated, *Never doubt that a small group of thoughtful, committed citizens can change the world; indeed, it's the only thing that ever has.* This quote serves as an inspiring reminder that even a few people can make a difference in the world. Whether it's working to end poverty or fighting for social justice, we all have the power to make a positive impact on our communities and beyond. It is important to remember that no matter how small our efforts may seem, they can still have a lasting effect on society. We should never underestimate the power of committed individuals who are passionate about making a difference and strive to create meaningful change in their communities. With dedication and hard work, we can all be part of something bigger than ourselves and help shape the future for generations to come.

Social Change Requires a Comprehensive Effort

What is it about the 60s and 70s that makes me wax poetic, besides the obvious fact of their being eras of immense transformation? It's not just because these decades provided us with some of the most inspiring examples of people coming together to fight for a better world. It's also not just because the music of these decades became anthems for movements, providing us with a soundtrack for our struggles. This era reveals the dramatic difference between those with wealth and those without, a discrepancy that has been amplified since the 1970s due to economic policies favoring affluent individuals. The last few decades also have seen a deeply entrenched system of racism, sexism, and other forms of discrimination that has caused dramatic inequality in wealth and access to resources.

What is solidarity and why is it important? Have you ever heard of a barn raising? A barn raising was a collective action of a community, in which a barn for one of the members was built. It was an event where everyone in the community would come together and help build the barn. This was important because it allowed people to work together and create something that would benefit the entire community. It also showed how powerful working together can be, as it allowed people to build something that would take much longer if done alone. Solidarity is the same concept as barn raising. It is when individuals or groups come together to work towards a common goal, and it is essential for collective action and social change. Through solidarity, individuals can join forces to overcome oppression, poverty, and injustice. It creates a sense of strength and unity, and it can be used to combat the systemic inequalities that exist in our society.

What is a Solidarity Economy?

Solidarity economy is a term that was coined in the 1970s that refers to a set of economic practices, structures, and processes based on principles of cooperation, equity, democracy, and sustainability. In the solidarity economy, people work together in collective efforts to achieve social and economic objectives that are beneficial for everyone. This includes cooperative businesses and networks, social and economic justice movements, public policies that promote economic democracy, and other strategies for creating an economy that works for everyone.

For decades, our society has been plagued by racism, sexism, and other forms of bigotry that have generated a vast disparity in financial well-being and access to resources. The traditional economic system can sometimes lead to the oppression of vulnerable individuals and resources, but solidarity economies provide a viable alternative. To build community wealth, we need to level the playing field and create opportunities for everyone to participate. We must ensure that everyone has a voice in decision-making and that the resources of our community are used for the benefit of all.

The solidarity economy is a global movement that seeks to create a just and sustainable economy where people and the planet are prioritized over endless profit and growth. It rejects state-dominated or billionaire-run systems in favor of cooperative, collective, democratically-controlled enterprises. This type of economy encourages collaboration between individuals, organizations, businesses, and projects with shared values such as equity, sustainability, justice, mutual aid, democracy, self-management, and interdependence.

By investing in solidarity economies around the world, we can create more equitable societies where everyone has access to basic needs such as food security, healthcare services, and education. Through this approach, we can also reduce poverty levels while protecting our environment from further damage caused by unsustainable practices.

Understanding Wealth Inequality and Other Societal Challenges

This book, Empowering Communities, explores the concept of the solidarity economy and how it can be applied to address issues of wealth inequality and other societal challenges in the 21st century. By understanding the history, philosophies, and practices of this economic model, you will gain an appreciation for its potential to create positive change in your local communities as well as in a global context. Through examining various strategies for building community wealth and fostering cooperation among disparate groups, you can gain an understanding of how to create a more just and equitable society.

The topics discussed include the impact of wealth inequality on global economics, ways to increase access to resources through cooperatives and networks, practices for leveling the playing field between participants, and approaches to ensure everyone has a voice in decision-making. You will also learn how to foster a culture of fairness, mutual respect, and cooperation in the workplace. By taking an inclusive and holistic view of the solidarity economy, this book provides an invaluable tool for understanding the complexities of wealth and its potential to transform our societies.

Community Wealth Building Values and Principles

Community wealth building (*via solidarity economy principles*) is not achieved through anarchy. On the contrary, it works best when governed by a set of principles and laws. Community wealth building is a people-centered economic development model that seeks to transform local economies by giving communities direct ownership and control of their resources. It is based on a set of values and principles such as equity, culture, mutuality, and stewardship. These principles are essential for successful community wealth-building as they provide clear guidelines on how to use economic resources, build wealth, share profits, and even organize labor unions.

Moreover, decisions must be made in an egalitarian manner with everyone having an equal say in decision-making processes. This ensures that all members of the community benefit from the collective efforts of the group. Additionally, it is important to ensure that there are mechanisms in place to prevent any one person or group from taking advantage of others within the community. Community wealth-building requires strong leadership and collaboration between different stakeholders to ensure its success. By following these principles and guidelines for community wealth building, we can create a more equitable society where everyone has access to economic opportunities and resources. This will lead to greater prosperity for all members of the community as well as increased social cohesion.

Capitalism and the Solidarity Economy

Can capitalism coexist with community wealth building via solidarity economy principles? The answer is yes, but it requires a shift in the way we think about and practice economics. Solidarity economy principles are based on the idea of shared ownership, cooperation, and mutual aid. This means that instead of relying solely on market forces to drive economic activity, people come together to create their own economic systems that prioritize collective well-being over individual profit.

Solidarity economy principles can be applied in a variety of ways. For example, cooperatives are businesses owned and operated by their members who share the profits and losses among themselves. They also often have democratic decision-making structures which allow for greater participation from all members. Another example is mutual aid networks which provide support to members during times of need without expecting anything in return.

The key to making solidarity economy principles work is to build strong networks of trust between individuals and organizations. This requires creating an environment where everyone feels safe to share ideas and resources without fear of exploitation or competition. It also requires recognizing the value of each person's contribution so that all members benefit from the collective effort.

Ultimately, solidarity economy principles offer an alternative approach to economic activity that puts people before profits and encourages collaboration over competition. By embracing these principles, we can create a more equitable society where everyone has access to the resources they need to thrive.

If This Book Were to Have a Soundtrack

The 60s and 70s were a time of great social change, and the music of the era captured this movement in powerful ways. I would be remiss if I didn't mention the enduring music of these artists who used their lyrics to inspire and motivate people to take action. The words they sang still resonate today, reminding us that each of us has a role to play in the fight for social justice and equity. If this book were to have a soundtrack, the following songs would be its most fitting accompaniment:

Introduction: Marvin Gaye's *What's Going On* serves as a powerful reminder of the deep-rooted issues in our society, from prejudice and inequity to wealth discrepancies and environmental devastation. Together these societal obstacles constitute an interconnected web that we must strive to unravel.

Chapter One: *Everyday People* by Sly and the Family Stone speaks of unity and acceptance, two important aspects of solidarity. This song captures the idea that everyone has something valuable to contribute, regardless of their background or identity.

Chapter Two: *People Get Ready* by The Impressions is a call for unity among all people regardless of race or religion. Curtis Mayfield's lyrics urge us to come together and work towards a brighter future where everyone can live peacefully together without fear or prejudice.

Chapter Three: *Get Up, Stand Up* by Bob Marley & The Wailers has inspired generations to stand up for their rights and the rights of others who may be oppressed or marginalized. This song is an anthem for social change, and it continues to inspire people today to fight for what they believe in.

Chapter Four: *Fortunate Son* by Creedence Clearwater Revival was written in response to the wealthy elites who were able to avoid military service while sending poor people off to fight wars they had no stake in, and has become a timeless anthem for those who have been wronged by their government and society.

Chapter Five: *For What It's Worth* by Buffalo Springfield speaks to the power of standing up for what you believe in. Even after more than 50 years, it continues to be an anthem for those seeking change and justice in our world.

Chapter Six: *The Times They Are A-Changin'* by Bob Dylan resonates even today, as it speaks to the power of collective action in bringing about meaningful change. It is a reminder that we all have a responsibility to fight for justice and equality, no matter how daunting the task may seem.

Chapter Seven: Woody Guthrie's folk anthem *This Land Is Your Land* has become an unofficial national anthem, standing the test of time with its powerful message of common ownership and a shared future, regardless of where we were born or who we are as individuals.

Chapter Eight: *Which Side Are You On?* by Florence Reece is a powerful song that speaks to the human struggle of deciding whether or not to join a cause. Composed in 1931, this union rallying cry captures the dilemma of staying safe on the sidelines while others march forward together, risking everything.

Chapter Nine: John Lennon's song *Imagine* speaks of a world without the divisions of religion, possessions, and culture that lead to greed and war. Lennon uses repetition of the word *imagine* to emphasize his message of hope for a better world through our collective action.

Chapter Ten: *Mercy Mercy Me* by Marvin Gaye is a powerful plea for environmental awareness that was released long before the environmental movement gained traction, yet it speaks to the same issues of pollution and destruction caused by humans that are still relevant today.

Chapter Eleven: Aretha Franklin's song *Respect* is an anthem of empowerment and a call for equality. Released in 1967, the song quickly became a rallying cry for the Civil Rights Movement and has since become an international symbol of respect and admiration.

Chapter Twelve: *Banks of Marble* by Les Rice is a powerful folk song that speaks to the struggles of workers against economic injustice. Written in 1949, it paints a vivid picture of the exploitation and unfairness faced by those whose wages don't keep up with inflation.

Chapter Thirteen: *If I Were a Rich Man* from the classic Broadway play, Fiddler on the Roof, captures the struggle of a Jewish milkman to make ends meet in czarist Russia. It's a reminder to us all that even when life is hard, we can still find joy in our circumstances and hope for better days ahead.

Chapter Fourteen: *We Shall Overcome* by Pete Seeger is an anthem of hope and resilience in the face of adversity, and serves to remind us that we can remain strong in the face of challenges and eventually overcome all obstacles.

CHAPTER 1

Everyday People

Working Together for a Better Future

Everyday People by Sly and the Family Stone speaks of unity and acceptance, two important aspects of solidarity. This song captures the idea that everyone has something valuable to contribute, regardless of their background or identity.

The powerful lyrics of this song, released in 1968 during a time of great civil unrest in America, echoed a passionate plea for peace and justice. The band's culturally-diverse backgrounds served as a beacon of inclusivity during an era when diversity was still rarely seen in the United States, and their music further drove this message home.

Everyday People is a fitting accompaniment to the theme of this chapter, and everyday people are the key to a sustainable system of community wealth and social change. It is only through understanding the needs and pains of our neighbors that we can create meaningful solutions. By understanding the individual motivations of everyday people, we can create a system that is beneficial to everyone.

Solidarity is a concept that underpins many efforts to create lasting change in our world today. It is a concept that reminds us that we are all connected and can only achieve real success when we work together. By recognizing our common humanity, we can move beyond hostile divisions and create an environment where everyone has equal access to resources, opportunities, and justice. Solidarity requires us to be open to the needs of our neighbors and understand the power dynamics that shape the lives of everyday people.

In this chapter, we will explore several inspiring instances of solidarity and how it can be utilized to create sustainable foundations for community wealth and social transformation.

The Poor People's Campaign

Rev. Dr. William J. Barber II is an American Protestant minister, social activist, professor in the Practice of Public Theology and Public Policy, and co-chair of the Poor People's Campaign: A National Call For Moral Revival. Rev. Barber has been likened to a contemporary Martin Luther King Jr. for his steadfast commitment and determination to social justice despite the opposition he receives from those who disagree with him. He has dedicated his life to fighting for equity and justice for all people regardless of race or economic status. His message of hope and unity resonates with many Americans today as they strive towards creating a better future for themselves and their communities.

Dr. Barber first gained national attention with his *Moral Mondays* protests in North Carolina, which called out systemic racism, poverty, ecological devastation, militarism, and the distorted moral narrative of religious nationalism. He has since become a powerful voice for change across the nation through his work with the Poor People's Campaign. Barber believes that solutions for injustice must come from those most affected by it and that everyday people have a responsibility to carry on their work. He encourages people to join together in a fusion coalition to challenge oppressive systems and create meaningful change in their communities. Rev. Dr. Barber's work with the Poor People's Campaign has been widely praised by activists and politicians alike as he continues his fight against injustice and inequality on behalf of all people regardless of their background or circumstances.

Since its inception in 2018, the Poor People's Campaign, established to honor Martin Luther King Jr.'s original 1968 campaign of the same name, has made great strides toward attaining its objective of eliminating systemic racism, poverty, and ecological destruction along with militarism and the war economy. Rev. Dr. Barber has been instrumental in leading this campaign by organizing rallies and protests across the country to bring attention to these issues and demand change from elected officials.

The Poor People's Campaign has achieved several important victories in recent years. In 2020, they engaged in talks with the incoming Biden-Harris administration about passing legislation that would raise the federal minimum wage to $15 an hour by 2025. They have also advocated for policies that would expand access to healthcare for low-income individuals and families as well as strengthen labor rights protections for workers across all industries. Additionally, they have worked with local governments to create more affordable housing options for those living in poverty and pushed for greater investment in public education systems nationwide.

ARISE (A Resource In Serving Equality)

ARISE is another grassroots organization that promotes the personal development and empowerment of the immigrant community, especially women, children, and youth living in the Rio Grande Valley. The organization does this by providing educational programs that help strengthen its community and civic participation. It was founded in 1987 by one woman, Sister Gerrie Naughton of the Sisters of Mercy order who went door-to-door in her new town of Las Milpas, Texas, meeting families to get a sense of the community's needs. She understood that for things to improve in her community, change needed to be led by the community members themselves—particularly the women of the community.

ARISE helps empower women by giving them a sense of purpose, and it also works to improve the town's conditions to help residents feel more dignified. ARISE has been networking with local businesses, nonprofits, and government organizations extensively. Along with proper plumbing, parks, and paved roads, the town now has several elementary schools and a nearby high school. It started with a single person and a handful of committed citizens from the local community. They were ordinary people who wanted to make their community a better place, not celebrities or wealthy individuals.

The National Domestic Workers Alliance (NDWA)

The National Domestic Workers Alliance (*NDWA*) is a national organization that works to promote the respect, recognition, and rights of domestic workers in the United States. Founded in 2007, NDWA is a powerful voice for more than 2.2 million nannies, house-cleaners, and home care workers across the country. NDWA is dedicated to creating a world where domestic work is valued and respected as dignified labor. They strive to build power among domestic workers by connecting them through exchanges and capacity-building initiatives. The organization also works to ensure that domestic workers have access to fair wages, benefits, safe working conditions, and basic labor protections.

To achieve its mission, NDWA engages in policy advocacy at the local, state, and federal levels; provides legal assistance; organizes campaigns; conducts research; and educates the public about the importance of recognizing domestic work as real work. They are led by an executive director and board of directors composed of current or former domestic workers from around the country. Through their efforts, NDWA has helped pass groundbreaking legislation that protects the rights of domestic workers in several states including New York and California. They have also been successful in raising awareness about issues such as wage theft and workplace discrimination faced by many domestic workers in the U.S., helping to create a more just society for all people who do this important work.

The Center for Popular Democracy (CPD)

The Center for Popular Democracy (*CPD*) is a progressive advocacy group that works to create equity, opportunity, and a dynamic democracy in partnership with high-impact base-building organizations. CPD is a federation of groups that includes some of the most influential grassroots community organizations in the United States, and is dedicated to advancing racial and economic justice. CPD engages in civic engagement, base-building, issue campaigns, and constituency mobilization to advance its pro-worker pro-immigrant, racial and economic justice agenda. They strive to build power through collective action by working with their partners to develop innovative policy solutions, win concrete improvements in people's lives, and build the strength of our movements for lasting change.

Through their work, they hope to make sure everyone has access to good jobs with fair pay; quality health care; safe consumer products; freedom from discrimination; retirement security; healthy environments; and strong public education. CPD has worked to pass legislation such as the Domestic Workers Bill of Rights in New York State which guarantees basic labor protections for domestic workers. They have also successfully advocated for increased funding for public schools and community colleges across the country. Additionally, CPD has been involved in campaigns to protect immigrant rights by advocating for sanctuary cities and fighting against deportations.

The Movement for Black Lives (M4BL)

The Movement for Black Lives (*M4BL*) is a coalition of more than 50 groups representing the interests of black communities across the United States. Founded in 2014, M4BL has created a popular strategy rooted in transformative goals that will impact the millions of Black people looking for direction and leadership in their fight against systemic racism and oppression.

M4BL has been at the forefront of many successful campaigns to bring attention to issues such as police brutality, mass incarceration, economic inequality, and voting rights. They have organized protests and marches around the country, held rallies and vigils to honor victims of police violence, and launched initiatives such as #BlackLivesMatter to raise awareness about racial injustice. Additionally, M4BL has worked with local governments to pass legislation that supports criminal justice reform and invests in communities of color. The Movement for Black Lives is an important part of the fight for racial justice in America. Through their work, they have helped bring attention to issues facing black communities, provided resources for activists on the ground, and pushed for meaningful change that will improve the lives of millions of people.

The Climate Justice Alliance (CJA)

The Climate Justice Alliance (*CJA*) is a collective of over 70 rural and urban community-based organizations focused on sustainability, environmental justice, and climate justice. CJA was formed in 2013 to create a new center of gravity in the climate movement by uniting frontline communities and organizations into a formidable force. Since its formation, CJA has achieved many significant victories against polluting and extractive industries. They have built local alternatives that center around the needs of frontline communities and are working to create a scalable, replicable model for grassroots organizing that can be used to fight for climate justice across the globe. CJA has also been successful in advocating for policy changes at both the state and federal levels, such as California's groundbreaking Environmental Justice Act of 2019. CJA is committed to creating a world where all people can live with dignity and respect, free from oppression and exploitation. Through their work, they are helping to build healthier communities from the ground up, while fighting for environmental justice and climate action everywhere.

The Right To The City Alliance (RTTC)

The Right To The City Alliance (*RTTC*) is a social movement that emerged in January 2007 as a response to the mass displacement of people due to gentrification, neoliberalism, and other forms of urban inequality. RTTC is a national alliance fighting for housing justice for all, against evictions, and advocating for renters' rights. Their goal is to build a national urban movement for housing, education, health, racial justice, and democracy by strengthening community organizations and creating transformative social movements.

Since its inception, RTTC has made significant strides in advancing its mission. They have developed campaigns such as the Homes For All campaign which works to end homelessness and create more affordable housing options. They have also worked with local governments to pass legislation that protects tenants from unjust evictions and rent increases. Additionally, they have organized rallies and protests to bring attention to issues of housing injustice and advocate for policy change. Overall, The Right To The City Alliance has been successful in its efforts to combat urban poverty and support cities in delivering sustainable development. Through their campaigns, protests, and legislative work they have helped create more equitable cities where everyone can access safe affordable housing.

The Indigenous Environmental Network (IEN)

The Indigenous Environmental Network (*IEN*) is a coalition of indigenous, grassroots environmental justice activists, primarily based in the United States. Founded in 1990, IEN's mission is to protect the sacredness of Mother Earth from contamination and exploitation by strengthening, maintaining, and respecting traditional teachings and natural laws. IEN works to build the capacity of Indigenous communities to develop economically and socially sustainable communities while protecting their environment. They provide resources such as grants, training programs, workshops, conferences, and more to help Indigenous people fight for their rights and protect their land. IEN also works with other organizations to promote environmental justice on a global level.

IEN has accomplished many things since its founding over 30 years ago. They have distributed over $200,000 USD in grants to Indigenous communities each year through their WMAN Grassroots Communities Mining Mini-Grant Program. They have also worked with organizations such as US Water Alliance and Transnational Institute to promote environmental justice on a global scale. Additionally, they are at the forefront of the global climate justice movement alongside other Indigenous movements. Overall, The Indigenous Environmental Network (*IEN*) is an important organization that works hard to protect the environment and promote environmental justice for Indigenous people around the world.

Partners for Dignity & Rights, formerly The National Economic & Social Rights Initiative (NESRI)

Partners for Dignity & Rights (*formerly The National Economic & Social Rights Initiative (NESRI)* is a nonprofit advocacy organization founded in 2004 with the mission of providing training, research, and lobbying on behalf of economic and social rights. NESRI works to build a broad movement for economic and social rights, including health care, education, housing, and work with dignity. NESRI has achieved numerous successes in its mission to promote economic and social rights. In 2005, NESRI was instrumental in the passage of the New York City Living Wage Law which ensured that workers employed by companies receiving city subsidies received wages sufficient to meet basic needs. In 2008, NESRI worked with community members in

New Orleans to pass an ordinance that would require all employers receiving public funds to pay their employees a living wage.

In addition to these legislative victories, NESRI has also been successful in advocating for policy change at the state level. In 2011, they successfully lobbied for the passage of California's Domestic Worker Bill of Rights which provided overtime pay and other protections for domestic workers in the state. They have also been involved in campaigns around issues such as payday lending reform and immigrant worker rights. NESRI continues to be an important voice advocating for economic and social rights both nationally and internationally. Through their work, they seek to ensure that all people are treated with dignity and respect regardless of their socioeconomic status or background.

National Housing Trust

The National Housing Trust (*NHT*) is a premier national nonprofit organization dedicated to preserving and developing affordable housing communities for low-income households. Founded in 1988, NHT works to equip communities for a sustainable, equitable future by preserving and modernizing existing homes—and building new ones that stand the test of time. NHT's accomplishments include providing loans and grants to finance, acquire, rehabilitate, and develop decent and safe affordable housing through the Texas Housing Trust Fund. The National Housing Trust Fund (*HTF*) is also focused on building, rehabilitating, preserving, and operating rental housing for extremely low-income people. Additionally, NHT has partnered with HUD to create the National Housing Trust Fund Factsheet which provides states with funds to expand the supply of affordable housing. NHT has been successful in its mission of creating more accessible housing options for low-income families. Through their efforts, they have provided thousands of families with access to safe and secure housing options at affordable prices.

Southern Partners Fund

Southern Partners Fund (*SPF*) is a 501(*c*)(*3*) public foundation that has been serving grassroots organizations in rural communities across the Southeast for over 20 years. SPF's mission is to provide these organizations with resources and support to help them achieve social, economic, and environmental justice. To accomplish this mission, SPF works with grantee organizations such as the Newtown Florist Club to provide funding for projects that promote desegregation. The organization also works with other philanthropic groups such as the Mary Reynolds Babcock Foundation and Astraea Lesbian Foundation For Justice to ensure that its grantees have access to the resources they need.

In addition, SPF has implemented a strategy of mission investing which allows it to use its funds in ways that will have a greater impact on social change. This includes investing in businesses that are committed to creating positive change in their communities and providing grants for projects that promote racial equity. Overall, Southern Partners Fund has had an impressive track record of success in helping grassroots organizations achieve their goals of social justice. Through its commitment to providing resources and support, SPF has been able to make a real difference in the lives of those living in rural communities across the Southeast.

Partnership for Working Families

The Partnership for Working Families (*PWF*) is a national network of leading regional advocacy organizations that are working to create innovative solutions to the nation's most pressing issues. PWF works with its 19 city and regional affiliates to build coalitions that have the power to transform our cities. Through their work, they provide hands-on research and technical assistance on community benefit agreements, organize to build community power, and ignite justice and progressive power.

PWF has made significant accomplishments in the areas of economic justice, racial equity, climate justice, and workers' rights. They have worked with local governments and communities to pass laws that raise wages for low-income workers, increase access to affordable housing and healthcare, protect immigrant rights, reduce carbon emissions from fossil fuels, create green jobs in renewable energy sectors, and more. These efforts have resulted in improved quality of life for many people across the country.

In addition to their work at the local level, PWF has also been involved in national campaigns such as advocating for an end to mass incarceration and police violence against Black people, fighting for fair wages, supporting labor unions, advocating for environmental justice, promoting gender equity, and protecting voting rights.

The Partnership for Working Families is now PowerSwitch Action—a bold new name that reflects their bold vision for multi-racial feminist leadership in building progressive power. With this new name comes a new website that provides resources on how individuals can get involved in their mission of creating equitable communities where everyone can thrive.

ROC United (Restaurant Opportunities Center)

ROC United is a not-for-profit organization and worker center that works to improve the lives of restaurant workers. Founded in 2002, ROC United has become the oldest and largest restaurant workers-led organization in the country. The organization's mission is to build worker power and unite restaurant workers of various backgrounds around shared goals and values.

ROC United has achieved many successes over the years, including fighting for higher wages, better working conditions, and more job security for restaurant workers across the country. In addition, they have successfully advocated for legislation such as the One Fair Wage Act which seeks to eliminate subminimum wages for tipped workers. They have also worked with employers to create new policies that promote workplace safety and provide better benefits for employees.

ROC United has also been successful in raising awareness about issues facing restaurant workers. Through their social media channels, they have been able to reach a wide audience with their message of fairness and justice in the workplace. They have also organized campaigns such as Diners United which encourages people to support restaurants that treat their employees fairly by dining at those establishments.

Overall, ROC United has had a significant impact on improving the lives of restaurant workers across the nation through its advocacy efforts and campaigns. By continuing to fight for fair wages, better working conditions, and more job security for all restaurant workers, they are helping to create a better future for those who work in this industry.

Movement Strategy Center

The Movement Strategy Center *(MSC)* is a 501*(c)(3)* nonprofit based in Oakland, California that has been challenging systemic racism since 2001. MSC provides values-aligned infrastructure for BIPOC and women-led organizations at the intersection of racial inequity and environmental justice. MSC works with grassroots organizations, alliances, and networks, as well as funders, to build powerful and transformative social justice movements. It provides space for reflection, experimentation, incubation, and fiscal sponsor services to BIPOC, women, and other marginalized communities.

MSC has had many accomplishments over the years. For example, it has helped launch several successful campaigns such as the California Environmental Justice Alliance *(CEJA)*, which is a statewide alliance of frontline environmental justice organizations working together to achieve environmental health and justice for all Californians. Additionally, MSC has also provided funding to support community organizing efforts in cities across the United States. Overall, The Movement Strategy Center is an important organization that is helping to create positive change in our society by providing resources to those who need them most.

Coalition on Human Needs

The Coalition on Human Needs *(CHN)* is a national alliance of organizations that are dedicated to promoting public policies that address the needs of low-income and vulnerable people in the United States. Founded in 1981, CHN is a non-partisan coalition of over 100 national organizations representing a broad range of constituencies, including civil rights, labor, faith-based, anti-hunger, and healthcare groups. CHN works to ensure that all people have access to necessities such as food, housing, healthcare, and education. The organization advocates for policies that will reduce poverty and inequality, protect vulnerable populations from discrimination and exploitation, and promote economic security for all Americans. CHN also works to ensure that federal programs are adequately funded so they can effectively serve those who need them most.

In addition to advocating for policy change at the federal level, CHN works with state and local partners to advance their initiatives. Through its network of partner organizations across the country, CHN has been able to help pass legislation that has improved access to healthcare services in many states. It has also worked with local governments to increase funding for affordable housing projects and other initiatives aimed at helping low-income families.

In recent years, CHN has worked closely with Congress on several major pieces of legislation related to poverty reduction and economic security. These include the Affordable Care Act (*ACA*), which expanded access to health insurance coverage; the Tax Cuts & Jobs Act (*TCJA*), which provided tax relief for low-income households; and the American Rescue Plan (*ARP*), which provided additional financial assistance during the COVID-19 pandemic. Through its advocacy efforts, CHN has helped millions of Americans gain access to vital resources they need to live healthy lives. The organization continues its work today by advocating for policies that will reduce poverty and inequality while protecting vulnerable populations from discrimination and exploitation.

National People's Action Campaign

The National People's Action Campaign (*NPAC*) is a coalition of more than 400 peace groups that was founded in 1982 to promote peace and justice. NPAC has been successful in achieving its goals by engaging in grassroots activism, organizing protests, and advocating for social change. NPAC's main focus is on issues such as poverty, racism, and militarism. The organization has organized numerous rallies and marches to raise awareness about these issues and to call for action from government officials. For example, NPAC organized a march in Washington D.C. in 1983 to protest U.S. military intervention in Central America and the Caribbean Basin. This march drew over 100,000 people from across the country and resulted in Congress passing legislation to limit U.S. involvement in the region.

In addition to organizing protests, NPAC also works with local communities to create economic opportunities for those living in poverty-stricken areas. The organization has worked with community leaders to create job training programs, small business development initiatives, and other projects that help individuals gain access to resources they need to improve their lives. NPAC has also been successful in advocating for changes at the national level as well as at the state level. In 2020, NPAC helped pass legislation that increased funding for public education and provided tax relief for low-income families across the country. Overall, NPAC has been successful in achieving its mission of promoting peace and justice through grassroots activism and advocacy efforts at both the local and national levels.

Equal Rights Advocates

Equal Rights Advocates *(ERA)* is a non-profit gender justice/women's rights organization that has been fighting for the rights of women, girls, and people of all gender identities since 1974. ERA works with advocates and community organizations across the United States to ensure that everyone has access to a fair paycheck, a safe and equitable workplace, and economic and educational opportunities.

ERA has achieved many successes in its fight for gender justice. They have successfully pushed for legislation such as the California Fair Pay Act which ensures equal pay for equal work regardless of gender or race. They have also provided legal representation to individuals who have experienced discrimination in the workplace or educational institutions. Additionally, they have researched issues related to gender equality and produced reports to raise awareness about these issues. ERA continues to fight for gender justice by advocating for policies that promote equity and inclusion in the workplace, education system, and beyond. They are committed to creating a just, free, and equitable society for all.

Women of Color Network, Inc.

The Women of Color Network Inc. *(WOCN)* is a national grassroots initiative that works to eliminate violence against women and families in communities of color. Founded in 1996, WOCN has been an advocate for the rights of women of color for over 25 years. WOCN's mission is to centralize the voices and promote the leadership of women of color who have experienced violence and oppression. They strive to create a safe space for survivors to share their stories and experiences, while also providing resources and support services to help them heal from trauma.

In addition to providing direct services, WOCN also works to raise awareness about the issues facing women of color through public education campaigns, advocacy efforts, and partnerships with other organizations. They have successfully advocated for legislation that protects victims of domestic violence and sexual assault, as well as increased access to mental health services for survivors. WOCN has also worked hard to build a strong network of allies who are committed to ending violence against all women and their communities. Through their work, they have helped countless individuals find healing and hope after experiencing trauma or abuse. By continuing its mission, WOCN hopes to create a world where all people can live free from fear and oppression regardless of gender or race.

350.org

350.org is an international environmental organization with a mission to end the use of fossil fuels and transition to renewable energy sources. Founded in 2008, 350.org has grown into a powerful grassroots climate movement with a presence in 188 countries around the world. Through online campaigns, grassroots organizing, and mass public actions, 350.org is inspiring people everywhere to take action on the climate crisis.

The organization has achieved many successes since its founding, including helping to stop the Keystone XL pipeline from being built and pushing for divestment from fossil fuel companies by universities and other institutions. In addition, 350.org has organized large-scale protests such as the Global Climate Strike in 2019 which saw millions of people around the world take part in demonstrations calling for urgent action on climate change. 350.org continues to work tirelessly towards its goal of ending the use of fossil fuels and transitioning to renewable energy sources that are better for our planet's future. By connecting powerful grassroots movements around the world and encouraging people everywhere to take action on climate change, 350.org is leading us toward a clean, just future that we can all be proud of.

Immigration Equality

Immigration Equality is the nation's leading LGBTQ and HIV-positive immigrant rights organization. For over 25 years, they have been fighting for safety and freedom for those facing discrimination in U.S. immigration law due to their sexual orientation or HIV status. They provide free legal services to individuals seeking asylum, as well as advocating for policy change to reduce the negative impact of immigration law on LGBTQ and HIV-positive people. Immigration Equality has achieved several successes since its founding in 1994. In 2010, they won a landmark case in the U.S. Supreme Court which allowed foreign same-sex partners of U.S. citizens to be eligible for green cards, allowing them to remain in the country legally with their families. In 2015, they successfully advocated for the passage of an executive order which provided protection from deportation for certain undocumented immigrants who had been living in the United States since 2010 or earlier.

In addition to providing legal services and advocating for policy change, Immigration Equality also provides education and outreach programs aimed at increasing awareness about LGBTQ and HIV-positive immigrant rights issues, as well as offering support services such as mental health counseling and financial assistance programs. Through their work, Immigration Equality has helped countless individuals achieve safety and freedom in the United States.

The Innocence Project

The Innocence Project is a non-profit legal organization that works to exonerate individuals who have been wrongfully convicted, and to reform the criminal justice system to prevent future injustices. Founded in 1992, The Innocence Project has helped free over 375 innocent people from prison, many of whom had served decades for crimes they did not commit. The Innocence Project uses DNA testing to prove innocence when available and appropriate, while also working to reform the criminal justice system through policy changes and public education. They have achieved numerous successes in this regard, such as helping pass laws that allow for post-conviction access to DNA testing in all 50 states and the District of Columbia. They have also worked with law enforcement agencies across the country to develop best practices for eyewitness identification procedures.

The Innocence Project has chapters located throughout the United States, including The Innocence Project of Texas and Oregon Innocence Project. These organizations work on a local level to help free those wrongfully convicted in their respective states. The Innocence Project is committed to creating a more just society by ensuring that innocent people are not wrongfully imprisoned or executed. With their tireless efforts, they are making progress towards achieving this goal every day.

Sunrise Movement

The Sunrise Movement is a youth-led organization that is dedicated to fighting climate change and creating millions of good jobs in the process. Founded in 2017, the movement has grown rapidly, with over 800 hubs across the United States and a presence in countries around the world.

The Sunrise Movement has had numerous successes in its short history. In 2018, they helped pass the Green New Deal resolution in Congress, which proposed sweeping changes to reduce emissions and create green jobs. They have also organized massive protests and rallies to raise awareness about climate change and advocate for environmental justice. Additionally, they have launched campaigns to pressure corporations and governments to take action on climate change.

The Sunrise Movement is an inspiring example of how young people can make a difference on issues that affect us all. Through their activism, they are helping to create a better future for generations to come.

United We Dream

United We Dream (*UWD*) is the largest immigrant youth-led network in the United States. Founded in 2008, UWD has grown to a membership of over 1 million people, with 25 local hubs across the country. In 2012, UWD successfully advocated for President Obama's Deferred Action for Childhood Arrivals (*DACA*) program, which allowed undocumented immigrants who arrived in the U.S. as children to remain in the country without fear of deportation. In 2017, UWD launched its #HereToStay campaign, which aimed to protect DACA recipients from potential deportation under the Trump administration. The campaign was successful and DACA remains intact today. UWD also works to empower immigrant youth through education and leadership development programs such as their Dream Summer Internship Program and their Dreamer Civic Engagement Program. Through these initiatives, UWD provides young people with resources and support to become active members of their communities and advocates for change.

Undoubtedly, many more grassroots organizations have been formed and run by everyday people working together for a better future. In most cases, they started with one or more passionate individuals who had an idea and the determination to make it a reality. Their collective efforts have driven positive change in their respective communities, and they are a testament to what can be accomplished with vision and dedication.

CHAPTER 2

People Get Ready

Practicing Enlightened Self-Interest

People Get Ready by The Impressions is a call for unity among all people regardless of race or religion. Curtis Mayfield's lyrics urge us to come together and work towards a brighter future where everyone can live peacefully together without fear or prejudice.

People Get Ready still resonates deeply with many people today as they demand justice for Black lives. At its core, *People Get Ready* is about faith and resilience in the face of adversity. It encourages people to believe in a better future, even when progress seems impossible. Ultimately, this timeless message teaches us that patience and determination can bring about real change—for individuals and communities alike.

Overcoming fear and division and getting organized is the theme of this chapter and is an essential aspect of building equitable, healthy, and thriving communities. It outlines strategies for fostering collective action within and across communities—while honoring individuality and protecting human rights. As you saw in chapter one, several organizations are doing great work to fight inequality. We can support them with our time, energy, and money. We can also join forces with like-minded individuals to create our own organizations. But, we can't sit back and wait for someone else to fix the problem. There is strength in numbers, and the more people we have working together, the more we can accomplish.

Getting Organized

When you think of community organizing, what comes to mind? If you're like most people, you probably imagine groups of protesters rallying for a cause. While protesting can be an important form of community organizing, it's only one small part of a much larger movement.

Community organizing is about empowering people to come together and make positive changes in their communities. Most people want to make a difference in their communities, but they often don't know where to start. That's where community organizing comes in. By coming together and sharing their stories and experiences, community members can identify the problems they want to address and develop creative solutions to make those changes happen.

Organizing can also help build relationships between people who might not otherwise have a chance to connect. When we come together and work towards a common goal, we can learn more about each other and build relationships of trust and understanding. These relationships are what bind us together as a community and help us weather difficult times.

Organizing was a way to make progress in the early 20th century. It also helped protect immigrants and minorities from being unfairly targeted and deported. The labor movement was able to make significant progress in improving working conditions and wages by organizing. The civil rights movement used organizing to end segregation and advance equality. Women's rights, LGBTQ rights, and environmental justice movements have all used organizing to achieve their goals.

Today, we need to continue this tradition. We need to get involved and stay involved. The only way to create lasting change is to keep up the pressure. Organizing is a way to help people create the social movements and political organizations necessary to wage campaigns and win power. We can't do this alone. We need to work together, build strong relationships, and stay organized.

With all the challenges that we face today, it is important to remember that organizing isn't just about making change—it's also about building community. When we come together to fight for justice and create a more equitable society, we are also creating a sense of belonging and community. We can come together to celebrate our successes, support each other through struggles, and create the world we want to live in.

Americans are known for being self-reliant. It is a fundamental principle of our nation. We are founded on the idea that all are created equal and that we have the right to life, liberty, and the pursuit of happiness. But, individualism and the free-market ideology that believes rewards are distributed according to merit also encourage people to think that their troubles are always their own fault.

If we don't challenge those views, the people will become demoralized and passive and few people will be willing to take the risk to take action. We need to remember that we are not alone. We are part of a long line of people who have fought for justice. We have tools at our disposal that they didn't have. We can use technology to connect and share information instantly. We can use social media to reach a wide audience. And we can use the Internet to organize people and resources.

Healing Divisions

The numerous divisions that exist in our society have been fostered over decades by those in power. To build wealth in the solidarity economy (*a community wealth-building system that puts people over profits*), we must first work to heal these divisions. One way to do this is by promoting racial and ethnic diversity within the solidarity economy. This includes but is not limited to people of color, women, LGBTQIA+ individuals, immigrants, and indigenous people. By making the solidarity economy more diverse, we make it more powerful. We also make it more reflective of the communities in which it exists.

However, it is worth noting that when attempting to build wealth in a community, there are many instances in which a homogeneous group of individuals has successfully done so. This is often the result of necessity, as in the case of many African American communities that were purposely isolated from the mainstream economy by racist housing and lending practices, or immigrant communities that were geographically isolated from it. The key is to ensure that the opportunity to build wealth in the solidarity economy is open to all, regardless of race, ethnicity, or any other dividing factor. In all cases, it is important to consider the unique needs of each community.

The adage, *The enemy of my enemy is my friend*, has been around for centuries and is still relevant today. It suggests that to achieve a common goal, it may be necessary to collaborate with someone who you don't necessarily like or agree with. This idea can be seen throughout history, from the alliances formed during World War II to the partnerships between companies in the modern business world. The concept of working together despite differences is an important one, as it allows for progress and growth that wouldn't otherwise be possible. By recognizing our shared humanity and understanding that we are all capable of achieving great things when we work together, we can overcome any obstacle.

In the community wealth-building movement, it's called the *solidarity economy*. This means that we must be willing to work with those who have different backgrounds or beliefs than we do. This is not to say that we should abandon our principles or values, but rather that we should be willing to engage in difficult conversations with those who may not share our worldview. Only by doing so can we hope to find common ground and build wealth together.

To build wealth in the solidarity economy, we must first understand that we are not alone. Many people and organizations are working towards the same goal. We must find allies in the fight against economic inequality, and we must work together to create change. One way to do this is by forming partnerships with organizations that have complementary goals. For example, a community development organization may partner with a cooperative business to provide training and technical assistance. By working together, we can create a more just and equitable society.

Practicing Enlightened Self-Interest

Enlightened self-interest is the idea that we should do things not just because they benefit us directly, but also because they lead to a greater good.

In other words, it's the recognition that what's good for society is also good for the individual. This may seem like a counterintuitive concept, but it has been endorsed by some of the most successful people in history.

One of the most famous advocates of enlightened self-interest was the American businessman and philanthropist Andrew Carnegie. In his 1889 essay *The Gospel of Wealth*, Carnegie argued that the rich must use their wealth wisely to benefit society as a whole. Specifically, he advocated for using one's resources for *the improvement of mankind*, such as by funding education, medical research, and infrastructure projects.

This concept is particularly relevant when it comes to building wealth within a community. For a community to be prosperous, its members must not only look out for their own interests, but also work to benefit the community as a whole. When everyone works together for the common good, everyone's efforts add up to create a greater whole. Here are some ways that individuals and organizations can work together to build prosperity in their community :

Giving Back to the Community: One of the best ways to practice enlightened self-interest is to give back to the community that has helped you succeed. This can take many forms, from volunteering your time to donating money to charities. Giving back not only benefits those in need, but also strengthens the community as a whole. When you give back to your community, you are investing in its future. You are also sending a message that you care about more than just yourself; you care about the welfare of others as well.

Helping Others Can Make You Happier and Healthier: One of the best reasons to give back is that it can make you a happier and healthier person. When you give of your time, money, or expertise, you get an infusion of good feelings—called the *helper's high*. Those good feelings can lead to increased happiness, life satisfaction, and physical health. One study found that volunteering just two hours a week can be enough to increase your overall sense of well-being. So if you're looking for a way to boost your happiness and health, giving back is a great option.

Giving Can Create Opportunities for Networking and Career Advancement: Another benefit of giving back is that it can open up doors for networking and career advancement. When you volunteer or donate to a cause that's important to you, you'll meet like-minded people who can become valuable contacts. As your network grows, so does your potential for finding new job opportunities or advancing in your career. And since many employers value employees who are actively involved in their communities, giving back can also make you more attractive to potential employers.

Giving Back Can Enhance Your Sense of Purpose: Giving back can enhance your sense of purpose in life. When you dedicate yourself to a cause bigger than yourself, you'll find new meaning and satisfaction in your life. And as your sense of purpose gets stronger, so does your motivation to achieve your goals and live a fulfilling life. So if you're looking for ways to add more purpose to your life, look no further than giving back to your community.

Investing in Education: Enlightened self-interest dictates that we should invest in education not just for our own benefit, but also for the benefit of society as a whole. A well-educated population is better equipped to solve social and economic problems, and thus create a better world for everyone. Inequalities in wealth are exacerbated by a lack of educational resources. By making sure that everyone has access to quality education, we can help level the playing field and create a more just and prosperous society.

Promoting Economic Development: Promoting economic development is another way to practice enlightened self-interest. When businesses thrive, they create jobs and generate tax revenue that can be used to fund important public services like education and infrastructure. A thriving economy also benefits consumers, who have more money to spend on goods and services. By promoting economic development, we can create a virtuous cycle of growth and prosperity that benefits everyone.

Supporting Social Welfare Programs: Social welfare programs like food stamps and Medicaid provide vital assistance to low-income families and help reduce poverty. But these programs also benefit society as a whole by ensuring that everyone has access to the basic resources they need to live healthy, productive lives. In addition, social welfare programs promote economic stability by preventing people from falling into desperate circumstances. By supporting social welfare programs, we can show that we care about more than just our own interests.

Investing in Local Businesses and Entrepreneurs: By supporting local businesses, you are not only helping to create jobs and grow the economy, but you are also keeping your money within the community. This creates a positive feedback loop in which money circulates within the community, benefiting everyone. In addition, investing in local entrepreneurs helps to create new businesses and promote innovation. This is good for the economy and good for society as a whole.

Creating Opportunities for Others: This could mean mentoring someone who is looking to start a business, offering internships or apprenticeships at your company, or even just being a sounding board for someone with a great business idea. By sharing your knowledge and expertise, you can help others reach their potential and contribute to the community as a whole.

Supporting Community-Based Organizations: Many organizations work to improve the lives of those living in poverty or otherwise marginalized communities. By supporting these organizations, you are helping to ensure that they can continue their important work. In addition, you may be able to volunteer your time or donate money to these organizations. Either way, you will be making a positive impact on the community.

Promoting Social and Economic Justice: Enlightened self-interest also leads us to fight for social and economic justice. We cannot create a prosperous society if some members are left behind. By promoting policies that help those who are most vulnerable, we can create a more just and equitable society—one that benefits us all. Enlightened self-interest is a powerful force for good. By looking out for the interests of others, we can create a better world for everyone.

Summary: Enlightened self-interest is an important concept for anyone looking to build wealth within a community. By considering how our actions will impact others, we can make sure that we are not only working in our own interests, but also in the interests of our communities. When everyone works together towards the common good, everyone benefits—and that is what enlightened self-interest is all about.

Overcoming Fear

Unfortunately, our most popular worldviews—the major religions, national identities, and political ideologies—cause us to divide ourselves into tribes and see others as a threat. This worldview has led to much suffering throughout history, and it continues to do so today. The primary driver of this division is fear—fear of the other, fear of change, and fear of the unknown. It presumes that one group's benefits come at the expense of another.

As a way of coping with fear, humans created cultural worldviews that instill our lives with meaning and purpose, and give us a sense of permanence. Allegiance to a group's beliefs, standards, and rituals is a comfort to those in fear because it provides a sense of certainty.

Controlling the *other* is also a way of dealing with fear. When we feel threatened, we often seek to demonize and dehumanize those who are different from us. We see them as a source of our problems, and we want to get rid of them. This is the mindset that leads to war, genocide, and other forms of violence. It also translates into policies and practices that benefit one group over another.

Overcoming fear involves understanding its root causes, challenging negative and irrational beliefs, finding common ground to build wealth together, working together to create a more just and equitable society, and developing a growth mindset. If we want to achieve our full potential, we need to find ways to overcome the fear of *others*. Here are several ways to do just that.

Acknowledge the Fear: Acknowledging fear is the first step in overcoming it. When we recognize our fears and accept them, we can begin to take steps toward overcoming them. By understanding why we feel afraid and what triggers our fear, we can start to create strategies for managing our emotions and reactions. If you're scared of those who pose a threat to you, take a moment to explore the source of that feeling and comprehend what's causing it.

Understand that Everyone is Different: One of the reasons we may be afraid of someone we see as a threat is because they're different from us. Maybe they dress differently, talk differently, or come from different backgrounds. It can be difficult to understand why someone would have a different perspective than our own, but it's important to remember that everyone is unique and that those differences should be celebrated, not feared. We should strive to create an environment where everyone feels accepted and respected for who they are. By celebrating differences, we can foster respect and open-mindedness for other cultures and backgrounds. This helps unite us all in our common interests while also allowing us to appreciate the unique qualities each individual brings to the table.

See the Person for Who They Are: Seeing people for who they truly are can be difficult, especially when we let our fears get the best of us and create an image of someone that doesn't reflect reality. It's easy to jump to conclusions and make assumptions about a person's character or intentions, but it's important to take a step back and try to see them objectively. When we do this, we often realize that the person isn't as intimidating as we initially thought. It's also important to pay attention to body language and tone when interacting with someone. These subtle cues can give us insight into how someone is feeling and what their true intentions are. We should also be aware of our own biases and preconceived notions when interacting with others, as these can cloud our judgment and prevent us from seeing the person for who they really are. By taking the time to observe people objectively, without judgment or fear, we can gain a better understanding of who they are and how they view the world. This allows us to connect with them on a deeper level and build meaningful relationships based on mutual respect and understanding.

Talk to the Person: Talking to people can be intimidating, but it doesn't have to be. Once you get to know someone for who they are, you'll come to realize that there's no reason to be scared. Instead of worrying about the conversation, try to engage in meaningful dialogue and talk about your differences. You might even find that you have more in common than you thought. To make talking easier, focus on being curious and open-minded. Ask questions and listen attentively. Additionally, don't forget the power of a compliment or two! It can help break the ice and start a conversation off on the right foot. With these tips in mind, talking to people can become an enjoyable experience instead of something that causes anxiety. So take a deep breath and go out there—you never know what kind of connections you could make!

Seek Out Help If Needed: Seeking out help can be a great way to conquer fear and anxiety. If you find yourself struggling to overcome your fear on your own, don't hesitate to reach out for professional guidance. With the right help, you can learn how to manage and eventually overcome your fear and start living a life free from it. It's important to remember that you don't have to go through this alone; there are many resources available that can provide you with the support and guidance you need.

Practice Compassion: Practicing compassion is an essential part of being a good human being. Instead of seeing others as a threat, try to see them as fellow human beings who are going through their own struggles. By doing this, you can foster a sense of connection and understanding with those around you. Compassion is defined as the feeling that arises when confronted with another's suffering, coupled with an urgent desire to aid or spare them from it. It is more than just sympathy or commiseration; it involves actively engaging with the person in need and providing whatever help you can. Compassion also means recognizing that we all have our own struggles and that no one should be judged for theirs. By taking this approach, we can create a more inclusive and supportive environment for everyone.

Find Common Ground: Finding common ground with someone who may have initially made you feel threatened can be a powerful way to dissipate fear. Instead of seeing the person as a threat, try to identify things that you both have in common. This could be anything from shared interests or hobbies to similar values and beliefs. Once you find something that connects the two of you, it can help to create an atmosphere of understanding and acceptance, allowing the fear to start to fade away. Additionally, it is important to remember that fear is often based on assumptions or preconceived notions about another person—by taking the time to get to know them better, we can often discover that our initial fears were unfounded.

Work Together: Working together is one of the most important aspects of building trust and respect in the workplace. When we come together to work towards a common goal, it quickly becomes clear that we all have something to offer. This can help break down any barriers or preconceived notions that may exist between colleagues and create an atmosphere of collaboration and mutual understanding. By taking the time to listen to each other's ideas, opinions, and perspectives, we can foster an environment where everyone feels heard and respected. Additionally, honoring commitments and being honest with each other will further strengthen the sense of trust within the team. With these steps in place, teams can be more productive and successful in achieving their goals.

Develop a Growth Mindset: Developing a Growth Mindset is essential for success. It means that instead of seeing others as a threat, you view them as an opportunity to learn and grow. This shift in perspective can have a tremendous impact on your life. With a growth mindset, you are more likely to take on challenges and learn from them, increasing your abilities and achievement. You also become more open to feedback and criticism, allowing you to improve yourself and reach new heights. Developing a growth mindset can help you to become more confident and comfortable in your own skin, allowing you to become the person that you want to be.

Be the Change You Want to See: If you want to see a world where people are more accepting of others, start by being more accepting yourself. To do this, it is important to understand where others come from and put yourself in their shoes. We should remember that we are all different and should think before we speak. Look for the positive in each situation and live in the present moment. Try to be compassionate and don't be quick to judge. It is also important to practice acceptance by noticing our own resistance and questioning our patterns. Lastly, show appreciation for those around us and be compassionate towards them. By doing these things, we can lead by example and show others that it is possible to overcome the fear of those we see as a threat.

Ultimately, overcoming fear is an essential part of being successful in our increasingly diverse world. We need to be able to embrace differences and work together towards common goals. With enlightened self-interest and understanding of others, we can move beyond our fears and build a more inclusive and prosperous future. When we show up with compassion and understanding, rather than fear and suspicion, amazing things can happen.

CHAPTER 3

Get Up, Stand Up

The Principles and Values of Solidarity

Get Up, Stand Up by Bob Marley & The Wailers has inspired generations to stand up for their rights and the rights of others who may be oppressed or marginalized. This song is an anthem for social change, and it continues to inspire people today to fight for what they believe in.

As we saw in chapter one, several organizations are doing great work to fight inequality. We can support them with our time, energy, and money. We can also join forces with like-minded individuals to create our own organizations. But, we can't sit back and wait for someone else to fix the problem. There is strength in numbers, and the more people we have working together, the more we can accomplish. To appreciate the opportunities that a solidarity economy offers, it is necessary to have a good understanding of the principles and values that underpin it. These elements include cooperation, solidarity, sustainability, and social and economic justice. Solidarity economics is an alternative to the current capitalist system that prioritizes profit over people and the planet.

Sustainability

The solidarity economy is based on the principle of sustainability, which means that we use resources in a way that meets the needs of current generations without compromising the ability of future generations to meet their own needs. This contrasts with the extractive, exploitative mindset of the capitalist economy, which sees natural resources as nothing more than commodities to be extracted and consumed. There are many different ways to practice solidarity economics, but all of them share a few key values. First and foremost, solidarity economics prioritizes people and the planet over profit. This means that decisions about what to produce, how to produce it, and for whom to produce it are made based on meeting human needs and protecting the environment, rather than on maximizing financial gain.

Cooperation

The solidarity economy is based on the principle of cooperation, which means that individuals and groups work together to achieve a common goal. This contrasts with the individualistic, competitive mindset of the capitalist economy, which pits people against each other in a race to the bottom. In a solidarity economy, businesses work together for the common good, rather than trying to undercut each other or drive each other out of business. This cooperative approach extends beyond businesses to include workers as well—solidarity economics envisions a future in which workers own and control their workplaces collectively.

Social and Economic Justice

The solidarity economy is based on the principles of social and economic justice, which means that everyone in a community should have access to the resources they need to live a dignified life. This contrasts with the unequal, exploitative nature of the capitalist economy, which concentrates wealth and power in the hands of a few. Solidarity economics strives for economic democracy—that is, decision-making power over economic activity should be vested in communities rather than in large corporations or institutions. One way this can be accomplished is through worker cooperatives, which are businesses owned and operated by the people who work there.

Solidarity

The solidarity economy is based on the principle of solidarity, which means that members of a community help each other out and look out for each other. This contrasts with the atomistic, self-interested mindset of the capitalist economy, which encourages people to look out for only themselves. For example, the principle of cooperation provides opportunities for individuals and groups to work together to create something bigger and better than they could on their own. The principle of solidarity provides opportunities for members of a community to help each other out and look out for each other. And the principle of sustainability provides opportunities for us to use resources in a way that meets the needs of current generations without compromising the ability of future generations to meet their own needs.

How to Build a Solidarity Economy

The Solidarity Economy movement is still in its early stages, but there are several things that individuals and groups can do to support and build the Solidarity Economy.

Support Local Businesses: One way to build the Solidarity Economy is by supporting local businesses. When you buy from locally owned businesses, you keep your money circulating in your local community, which strengthens the local economy. In addition, locally owned businesses are typically more responsive to the needs of their community and are more likely to give back to the community through charitable giving and other forms of social responsibility.

Cooperate, Don't Compete: In the conventional economy, businesses are always trying to get ahead of their competitors by undercutting them on price or offering a better product or service. This type of competition often leads to negative outcomes such as job losses, wage stagnation, and environmental degradation. In contrast, cooperation is based on the principle that we all do better when we work together. When businesses cooperate, they can pool their resources and knowledge to create positive outcomes for everyone involved. For example, cooperative business models such as worker-owned cooperatives allow employees to share in the profits of the business, which gives them a vested interest in its success.

Invest in Your Community: When you invest in your community, you are supporting its long-term economic stability and resilience. One way to invest in your community is by becoming a member of a local credit union or community development financial institution *(CDFI)*. These types of institutions provide loans and other financial services to small businesses and low-income individuals who might not otherwise have access to capital.

Advocate for Policy Change: Attempting to influence policy change at the local, state, and federal levels is another approach to creating a solidarity economy. There are several ways to get involved in advocacy efforts, such as writing letters or making phone calls to your elected officials, attending rallies or protests, or donating money to support organizations that are working for change.

The principles of the solidarity economy—solidarity, cooperation, sustainability, and community-based investing—provide a values-based framework for creating an economy that works for everyone, not just the wealthy few. By supporting local businesses, investing in your community, and advocating for policy change, you can help build a solidarity economy in your community.

Taking Action to Build a Local Solidarity Economy

Taking action might begin with a single person, but it can also benefit from the aid of a few dedicated community members. With the appropriate mindset and playbook, a core group of community members may apply the concepts of organizing and building community wealth.

Over time, these practices can have a large impact on the social and economic makeup of a region. Organizing for change in the community is a process that takes time, energy, and dedication. It is not a quick fix, but it is an important step in the journey to creating a more just and equitable society. The following are some tips for organizing in the community:

Know Your Community: It is important to get to know the people in your community and understand their needs. This can be done by talking to people, attending community meetings, and conducting surveys. If you want to carry out an intervention or build a coalition, it is more likely to be successful if you understand the culture of the community and the relationships among individuals and groups within it.

Find a Community Issue that You are Passionate About: Once you know the needs of your community, you can begin to identify the issues that you are most passionate about. It is important to choose an issue to which you are willing to dedicate time and energy. Servant leaders are not born, they are made. Anyone can become a servant leader. All it takes is a commitment to serving others and making a difference in your community.

Develop Relationships: Building relationships takes time, patience, and effort. It's important to remember that you're not just trying to get people to like you—you're trying to develop relationships that will help you achieve your goals. Spending time with the people in your community should be enjoyable. If it's not, then you're likely to burn out quickly and won't be as effective in achieving your goals.

Build a Team: Organizing is more effective when it is done as a team. As you begin to organize, it is important to find other people who are passionate about the same issue. You can build a team by reaching out to friends, family, and neighbors. Selecting team members who have different skills, abilities, and experiences can also be helpful.

Develop a Coalition: Coalitions can be very effective in creating change because they bring together different perspectives and skills. These allies could be individuals, groups, businesses, or other organizations. Coalitions differ from teams in that they are usually larger and more diverse. Coalitions can be very effective in creating change because they bring together different perspectives and skills.

Develop a Plan: Once you have a team, you can begin to develop a plan of action. This plan should include a goal, a strategy, and a timeline. It is important to be realistic in your planning and to consider the resources that you have available. A good plan will also take into account the potential for opposition and have a contingency plan in place.

Take Action: Once you have a plan, it is time to take action. This might include holding community meetings, conducting research, writing letters, and organizing protests. Starting your planning with SMART goals will increase the chances of reaching the overall goal and gaining momentum by taking a series of smaller, short-term steps. SMART means goals that are specific, measurable, attainable, relevant, and time-based.

Evaluate Your Progress: As you take action, it is important to evaluate your progress and make changes to your plan as needed. This will help you to gauge your success and make necessary adjustments. Celebrate your successes and learn from your failures.

Organizing in the community is a vital step in the journey to creating a more just and equitable society. It is important to remember that servant leadership is not about one person being in charge. It is about working together as a team to make a difference. Anyone can be a servant leader. All it takes is a commitment to serving others and making a difference in your community.

The Power of Planning and Community Development

Too often, low-income neighborhoods and communities of color are left out of the conversation when it comes to planning and community development. This has led to a lack of investment in these areas, which has in turn led to disinvestment and disarray. But there is hope.

By getting organized and mobilizing, residents of these communities can begin to level the playing field and create real change. Residents need to be informed about the planning and development process so that they can be better prepared to participate in it. They also need to understand the impact that planning and development can have on their community. Once residents are armed with this knowledge, they can begin to get involved in the planning and development process in their own community.

Communities are constantly changing and evolving, but not always for the better. For residents to influence the direction of development in their communities, they must be proactive. By taking the initiative to reach out to local officials, attend community meetings, and get involved with local organizations, residents can ensure that their voices are heard and that they play a role in making their community a better place to live. Here are some specific ways that residents can get involved in the planning and development process:

Reach Out to Local Officials: Residents can connect with their local officials to discuss the improvements they would like to see in their community. They can do this by attending community meetings, sending letters or emails, or calling their offices. When meeting with officials, it is important to be respectful and come prepared with possible solutions. For example, if a resident would like to see more green space in their community, they could suggest that a vacant lot be turned into a park. To make an impact, residents should try to get involved with as many officials as possible and encourage their friends and neighbors to do the same.

Attend Community Meetings: Most communities have regular meetings open to the public. This is a great way for residents to stay up-to-date on current development projects and voice their opinions about proposed changes. If a resident cannot attend the meeting, they can often find meeting minutes posted online. Examples of community meetings include city council meetings, community board meetings, and public hearings. You can find out when and where these meetings are taking place by searching online or contacting your local officials.

Get Involved with Local Organizations: Many organizations are dedicated to improving conditions within specific communities. By getting involved, residents can help these groups achieve their goals while also ensuring that the changes made benefit everyone in the community. Examples of local organizations include neighborhood associations, block associations, and community development corporations. Most of these groups welcome new members and are always looking for volunteers.

Form a Community Organization or Coalition: This will allow residents to pool their resources and have a greater impact on the planning and development process. Community organizations can also help residents access government funding for projects that will benefit the community as a whole. Coalitions consist of representatives from different groups who work together to achieve a common goal. For example, a coalition could be formed to advocate for more affordable housing in a community.

Get Involved with Your Local Government: This can be done by attending city council meetings, contacting your representatives, or serving on a board or commission. There are many different ways to get involved, so find the one that best suits your interests and skills. For example, if you are concerned about the environment, you could serve on a green infrastructure commission. Or, if you want to help shape the future of your community, you could join a planning commission.

Get to Know Your Neighbors: Getting involved in neighborhood associations and other community groups is a great way to get to know your neighbors and the issues that are important to them. This can help build relationships and trust, which is essential for effective community development. Additionally, when residents know each other, they are more likely to look out for each other and take action when something needs to be fixed. By working together, you can have a greater impact on the direction your community takes.

Volunteer: By giving back to your community, you can help make it a better place for everyone. There are many different ways to volunteer, so find one that interests you and get started today. For example, you can volunteer at a local food bank or soup kitchen, help clean up a park, or mentor a child. Or, you can donate your time to a local organization that is working to improve conditions in the community. Volunteers make a difference in their community, and the more people that get involved, the greater the impact will be.

Shop Locally: Local businesses provide jobs and contribute to the tax base, which helps fund important services like schools and police departments. So next time you need something, consider shopping at a local business instead of a big box store. You might pay slightly more, but your purchase will go a lot further in supporting your community. By shopping locally, you are also more likely to get better customer service and build relationships with the business owners. In return, the owners are likely to be responsive to the needs of their customers and the community.

Be an Advocate for Change: If you see an issue that needs to be addressed, don't be afraid to speak up and start working towards a solution. Remember, every voice counts! Don't wait for someone else to take action, but rather be the change you want to see in your community. You don't have to be an expert to make a difference—you just need to be passionate about the issue and willing to speak up.

Educate Yourself and Others about the Planning and Development Process: One of the best ways to make sure your community is developed in a way that benefits everyone is to educate yourself and others about the process. By understanding how the planning and development process works, you can make sure that your community is being developed in a way that meets the needs of all its residents. While each community is different, there are some general steps that all communities go through when it comes to planning and development. For example, all communities need to go through a comprehensive planning process, which is used to create a vision for the future and identify goals and objectives. Next, zoning ordinances need to be created or updated to reflect the vision and goals of the community. Finally, development regulations need to be put in place to ensure that the vision is implemented in a way that is consistent with the community's goals.

The planning and development process can be complex, but it is important to understand how it works so that you can be an informed and engaged citizen. If you want to learn more about the planning and development process, there are many resources available, including books, websites, and articles. You can also attend community meetings or workshops, which are often open to the public. When it comes to community development, knowledge is power! By educating yourself and others about the process, you can make sure that your community is developed in a way that meets the needs of all its residents.

A Call to Action for Inclusive Leaders

It's always darkest before the dawn. This adage from the 1600s reminds us not to give up during hard times because things are the hardest right before they get better. The current state of diversity, equity, and inclusion (*DEI*) in America feels a lot like the darkness before the dawn.

There is no doubt that we have made progress in DEI over the past few decades. But the progress has been too slow and uneven. We still see too many organizations that lack basic inclusion practices, let alone advanced ones.

This is particularly true for organizations led by white men. Organizations aren't doing a good enough job of creating an inclusive environment, given the daily headlines about sexual harassment, unconscious bias, and racial discrimination.

The good news is that there is a growing movement of inclusive leaders who are committed to creating more diverse and inclusive organizations. These leaders come from all walks of life and all parts of the world. They are men and women, old and young, gay and straight, white and people of color. What sets inclusive leaders apart is their willingness to challenge the status quo, speak up for what's right, and take action to create change. They are the backbone of the DEI movement. If you're an inclusive leader, we need you now more than ever. We need you to continue speaking up and taking action to create change. We need you to be the backbone of the DEI movement. If you're not an inclusive leader, then we need you to become one.

A Flicker of Light in the Darkness

After years of being in denial, some companies are finally starting to face up to the fact that they have a gender pay gap problem. And it's not just a few companies—according to a recent study, almost half of all businesses in the US have a gender pay gap. The problem is especially prevalent in the tech industry, where women are often paid less than their male counterparts for doing the same job. This was highlighted recently when it was revealed that Salesforce CEO Marc Benioff initially disputed the existence of any gender-based wage gaps at his company. But after an internal audit found that women were paid less than men at Salesforce, Benioff acknowledged the problem and said he would take steps to fix it. Equalizing pay wasn't an easy process, or a cheap one. Salesforce spent $3 million to bring women's salaries in line with men's, and it also increased its overall budget for raises by 9 percent.

It's not just big companies that have a problem with gender pay gaps, though. Small businesses are also often guilty of paying women less than men for doing the same job. In fact, a recent study found that 34 percent of small businesses in the US have a gender pay gap. One of the reasons that gender pay gaps exist is that women are often undervalued in the workforce. This is especially true in male-dominated industries like tech. The good news is that more and more companies are becoming aware of the problem and taking steps to fix it. This is a positive trend that needs to continue if we want to see real change in the way women are treated in the workplace.

It Goes Far Beyond Women and Pay

It's not just gender-based pay gaps that are hurting American businesses. We need to take off the blinders and denial around the issues of systemic racism, sexism, misogyny, ableism, homophobia, and transphobia in our workplaces. In these cases, we are still woefully behind in making any real progress. For example, a recent study found that only 1 percent of venture-funded tech startup founders are Black. And only 2 percent of startup founders are Latine. This is even though Black and Latin-American people make up 13.4 percent and 18.3 percent of the U.S. population, respectively. The lack of diversity in tech startups is a reflection of the larger problem in the tech industry, which has been accused of being exclusionary and discriminatory against people who are not white and male.

We need to reckon with the ways these systems of oppression show up in our organizations, and we need to do the hard work of dismantling them. This is not going to be easy, but it's necessary if we want to create workplaces that are truly inclusive and equitable for all. Organizations that have the will to hold up a mirror to themselves and reckon with their own complicity in these systems of oppression will be the ones that thrive in the years to come. How do we know this? Data show that more inclusive organizations outperform their peers on nearly every metric, from employee engagement to innovation to profitability. Why is this the case? Because organizations that embrace diversity and inclusion are tapping into a vast pool of untapped talent and potential. When we create truly inclusive workplaces, everyone wins.

We can no longer afford to ignore the problem of inequality in our workplaces. It's time for a reckoning. It's time to face up to the fact that we have a lot of work to do if we want to create workplaces that are safe and welcoming for everyone. It's time to take action and make real change.

What can you do to help create more inclusive workplaces? Here are a few ideas:

- Educate yourself and others about the systems of oppression that exist in our workplaces.

- Speak up when you see or hear something exclusionary, discriminatory, or offensive.

- Challenge your own assumptions and biases about people who are different from you.

- Make an effort to create opportunities for underrepresented groups to succeed in your workplace.

- Support organizations that are working to create more inclusive workplaces.

- Tune out the negative noise of social media that can breed division and hostility.

- Focus on building relationships with people from different backgrounds, experiences, and perspectives.

- Lift as you climb, and use your privilege and platform to create opportunities for others.

This is a call to action for businesses large and small to reckon with their own complicity in systemic racism, sexism, misogyny, ableism, homophobia, and transphobia in the workplace. We need to do the hard work of dismantling these systems of oppression if we want to create workplaces that are truly inclusive and equitable for all. When we all commit to doing our part, we can create workplaces that are truly inclusive and equitable for all. It's time for leaders to grow a backbone. It's time for a reckoning.

Educating Ourselves About Inequality

The first step is to educate ourselves and others about the issue of wealth inequality. We need to understand how the system is rigged in favor of the wealthy and how this affects us. We also need to understand our power and how we can use it to create change. The more people who understand the issues, the better.

We need to be able to articulate our shared values and goals. We need to be able to have intelligent conversations with people who may not agree with us. We need to be able to persuade them to see our point of view. And of course, face-to-face conversation is always the best way to connect with people and get them to see your point of view.

Unless you've been living under a rock for the past few years, you're probably aware that wealth inequality is a major problem in the United States. But what you might not realize is just how significant the problem has become. The top 1% of Americans now own more wealth than the bottom 90%. This concentration of wealth at the top is unprecedented in our history.

Wealth inequality isn't just a problem for those at the bottom of the economic ladder; it's a problem for everyone. When such a large portion of the population doesn't have any significant savings or assets, it becomes difficult for them to weather financial setbacks, take advantage of opportunities, or retire comfortably. This lack of financial stability can lead to increased crime rates, lower educational attainment levels, and poor health outcomes—all of which drag down our economy as a whole.

So what can we do about this problem? Education is always a good place to start. If we can raise awareness about the issue of wealth inequality and get more people talking about it, we can start to build support for policies that will help reduce inequality and create a stronger, more prosperous economy for everyone. To understand how to solve a problem, it's important to first understand how the problem started. So let's take a look at some of the key factors that have contributed to rising wealth inequality in America.

Structural Racism: Throughout American history, people of color have been systematically prevented from accumulating wealth. From redlining and racial covenants to mass incarceration and predatory lending practices, minorities have constantly been pushed to the margins while white people have been given a leg up. As a result, minorities are far less likely to own homes or have retirement savings—two key components of building long-term wealth.

Wage Stagnation: For decades now, wages have remained largely stagnant while costs have continued to rise. This means that Americans are working harder than ever but still can't make ends meet. The type of work that many Americans do has also changed; jobs in manufacturing and agriculture—which often provided good benefits and paid decent wages—have declined sharply while service-sector jobs have increased. These jobs tend to be low-paying and provide little opportunity for advancement, which makes it difficult for workers to save money and build long-term wealth.

Taxes—or More Specifically, the Lack Thereof: Our country's tax system used to be much more progressive than it is now, which helped reduce inequality by ensuring that wealthy individuals paid their fair share. However, over the past few decades, there have been continual cuts to taxes on capital gains and inheritances while taxes on work income have remained relatively flat. This has exacerbated inequality by making it easier for those who already have money to amass even more while doing nothing to help those who are struggling financially.

The issue of wealth inequality is complex and multi-faceted, but that doesn't mean we shouldn't try to do something about it. By educating ourselves and others about the origins of this problem, we can start to build support for solutions that will create a more prosperous economy for everyone—not just those at the top.

CHAPTER 4

Fortunate Son

The Rise of Wealth Inequality

Fortunate Son by Creedence Clearwater Revival was written in response to the wealthy elites who were able to avoid military service while sending poor people off to fight wars they had no stake in, and has become a timeless anthem for those who have been wronged by their government and society.

Over the past several decades, we have seen a dramatic shift away from democracy and toward oligarchy—a form of government in which power is held by a small number of wealthy elites. The oligarchy has manipulated the rules of the economy, deregulated industries, signed trade deals that favor corporations over workers, and slashed taxes on the wealthy. Our economy has become increasingly unequal, and our government has become less responsive to the needs of ordinary citizens.

Wealth Inequality and the Shrinking Middle Class

Chances are that you consider yourself to be in the middle class—nearly everyone in the United States does. But, it can be tricky to define the middle class, as people's perceptions of their social class can vary widely. You may define it by income level or wealth, or regard it as a function of occupational status and educational attainment. You also can consider it a state of mind or a set of aspirations reflected in your actions and choices. However you define it, the middle class is often associated with the following set of characteristics:

- A college education

- Professional or managerial occupation

- Owning a home

- Living in a suburban or urban area

- Two or more cars

- A relatively high income, but not in the top 5 percent

The middle class represents the American Dream—the belief that anyone, no matter their background or station in life, can succeed through hard work and determination. The American Dream has been a powerful motivator for people throughout our history. It is what drew millions of immigrants to our shores in search of a better life. And, it is what has inspired generations of Americans to strive for a better future. Our recent history is replete with examples of rags-to-riches stories of fortunes made in the land of opportunity, including Andrew Carnegie, John D. Rockefeller, Henry Ford, and Bill Gates.

Who was in the Middle Class in 2020?

Many organizations in both the public and private sectors have worked hard to define and measure income levels throughout time. Although the U.S. government doesn't have an official definition of middle-class income, the Pew Research Center considers a household to have *middle-income* if it's between 67% and 200% of the median household income. The median income is the level at which half of the population earns more and half earns less. The U.S. Census Bureau found that the 2020 median income for all households was $67,521. Using $67,521 as the base, the Pew definition of middle income would include households earning between $45,239 and $135,042.

But that range does vary by the size of the household. To be considered part of the middle class in 2020, a single American must have earned between

$22,792 and $68,036. A two-person household must have earned between $50,966 and $152,138, a three-person household must have earned between $60,072 and $179,320, and a four-person household must have earned between $71,751 and $214,182.

Who was in the Middle Class in 1975?

To help us understand what these ranges signify over the last several decades, let's look back to the mid-1970s and compare these figures to the present. In 1975, the median income for all households was $11,800, which equals $51,762 in 2020 dollars. To be considered part of the middle class in 1975, a single American must have earned between $14,125 and $42,164 in 2020 dollars, while a two-person household must have earned between $32,832 and $98,006, a three-person household must have earned between $41,391 and $123,554, and a four-person household must have earned between $46,581 and $139,048. Overall incomes have risen over time, as you can see. But, let's take a look at how household size has changed in comparison to income.

Between 1975 and 2020, the number of households of any size grew by 178 percent. Single-person households grew by 247 percent, while two-person households grew by 203 percent, three-person households grew by 156 percent, and four-person households grew by 141 percent. In other words, the most rapid growth in the U.S. population of wage earners occurred in lower-middle-class households. Pew Research Center analyses indicate that the proportion of American adults who reside in middle-income households has dropped from 61% to 51% over the last four decades. Since 1971, this reduction has proceeded at a gradual but steady rate, with each decade ending with a smaller percentage of people living in middle-income homes than the previous one.

Measuring the Cost of Living

In the same period, the cost of living has outpaced earnings. Soon after its creation by Congress in 1884, the Bureau of Labor Statistics (*BLS*) started to collect data on Americans' cost of living. It was only a century ago, in 1921, that the United States government began tracking a national Consumer Price Index (*CPI*), which was based on the cost of living in big cities. The CPI is still the most-quoted indicator of living costs today, documenting how costs have fluctuated over time. The CPI adjusts for inflation by tracking changes in the prices of a *market basket* of goods and services that Americans purchase, such as rent, food, transportation, and medical care. The BLS publishes a separate CPI for each major metropolitan area, which is then used to calculate cost-of-living differentials for specific regions.

The relationship between earnings and the cost of living was largely different in the past. Incomes grew faster than prices up until the early 1970s, giving workers more buying power year after year. But then something changed: Incomes began to stagnate while prices continued to rise rapidly. From 1975 through 2020, inflation-adjusted median earnings increased by 30%. At the same time, the dollar had an average inflation rate of 3.55% per year between 1975 and 2020, producing a cumulative price increase of 381.06%. This means that prices in 2020 are 4.81 times higher than average prices since 1975, according to the Bureau of Labor Statistics consumer price index.

Measuring Income and Wealth Inequality

Today's level of income and wealth inequality is not sustainable and is creating a society that is increasingly divided between the haves and the have-nots. In terms of the United States' population, income levels are generally expressed as quintiles *(fifths)*. A quintile is a term used in economics to describe an income that falls within one of five equal-sized groups, each with 20% of the population. The first quintile contains the lowest 20% of earners, while the fifth quintile contains the highest 20% of earners. Between 1975 and 2020, incomes for all quintiles rose on average, but most of this growth was driven by the extremely rapid increase in the top quintile of income. Between 1975 and 2019, annualized growth rates were 0.4% for the bottom quintile, 0.6% for the 2nd quintile, 0.7% for the 3rd quintile, 0.9% for the 4th quintile, and 1.5% for the top quintile.

The Gini index is a statistical measure of inequality that ranges from 0 *(or perfect equality)* to 1 *(or perfect inequality)*. A value of 0 would indicate that everyone in the United States earned the same amount of money, while a value of 1 would mean that one person earned all the money and everyone else earned nothing. Between 1975 and 2020, the Gini index for income in the United States increased by 0.110 from 0.359 in 1975 to 0.469 in 2020, meaning that income inequality increased during this period. In 2020, the top quintile of earners captured 51% of all income, while the bottom quintile earned only 3.4%. In 1975, by comparison, the top quintile captured less than 42% of all income, while the bottom quintile earned 5.6%.

The Rapid Rise of the Top 1%

Income growth has been faster for people in the top fifth of the income distribution. But, even within that quintile, income gains have been further concentrated. Income shares of the top 1% peaked during the 1920s, fell and stabilized over the next 50 years, and then started climbing again in the early 1980s. Over the past five decades, the top 1% of American earners have nearly doubled their share of pre-tax national income. In 1975, the top 1% captured 10.4% of national income, while the bottom 50% captured 20.4% of national income. By 2020, the wealthiest 1% of Americans were taking in 19.1 percent of national income, while the least well-off half had fallen to 13.6%. Americans at this level of income now earn almost 196 times more than the bottom 90 percent.

At higher levels of wealth, in addition to income, it can be helpful to consider your net worth. This is the value of what you own minus what you owe. In 2020, the Federal Reserve estimated that the median net worth of American households was $97,300. The top 10% of households had a net worth of $1,070,000 or more, and the top 1% of households had a net worth of $11,040,000 or more. In contrast, the net worth of the bottom 10% was negative, meaning they owed more than they owned. Over the past three decades, America's most affluent families have added to their net worth, while those on the bottom have dipped into *negative wealth*, meaning the value of their debts exceeds the value of their assets, according to National Bureau of Economic Research data.

The Emergence of the Ultra-Rich Class

Income and wealth inequality in the United States is not only growing, but some believe it has reached levels not seen since the early twentieth century. The term *ultra-rich* generally refers to those individuals with a net worth of $30 million or more. In 2018, there were an estimated 663,000 ultra-rich people in the world, and their combined net worth was $29.7 trillion. The United States is home to more ultra-rich people than any other country, with 155,000 ultra-rich individuals.

The ultra-wealthy not only have more money than everyone else, but they also have greater access to a variety of other assets. The Federal Reserve's Distributional Financial Accounts data reveal that most of their wealth comes from different types of assets, which are more lucrative. The top 1% of American households hold more than half of the entire stock and mutual fund assets in the country. In comparison, the majority of the wealth in the bottom 90 percent of Americans comes from their homes—an asset class that suffered the most during the Great Recession. About three-quarters of America's debt is also held by the bottom 90%.

The American Dream is Getting Crushed

The economic inequality that has characterized America for the past several decades has only grown wider in recent years, and the middle class has shrunk accordingly. The trend toward increased inequality is not unique to the United States. It is occurring in most developed countries. But the U.S. has been experiencing it at a much faster rate. The top 1% of Americans now own more wealth than the bottom 90%. This concentration of wealth means that there is less opportunity for upward mobility. The rules that once favored the middle class have been rewritten to favor the ultra-rich. And, as the middle class has shrunk, the power of the ultra-rich has grown.

The American Oligarchy has Returned

The concentration of income at the top is not just a recent phenomenon. It is strikingly similar to the income distribution of America in the early 20th century when the country was known as the *land of opportunity*. The period from roughly 1880 to 1920 was marked by rapid economic growth and increased opportunity for upward mobility. But it was also a time when the gap between the rich and the poor was widening. By 1920, the top 1 percent of Americans earned nearly 20 percent of all income—more than double their share in 1880.

This concentration of income at the top continued into the mid-20th century, but it began to reverse in the 1970s. The top 1 percent's share of income declined throughout the 1970s and 1980s, before reaching its lowest level since the early 20th century in 1988. Since then, however, it has been on the rise again. A 2016 Pew Research Center report found that 51 percent of adults in the U.S. say they are either *lower middle class* or *poor*. This is the highest share of Americans who have self-identified as low-income since the 1970s.

Today's ultra-rich, well-connected class of individuals control the country, frequently disregarding middle-class values and the majority of citizens' preferences. America's political and economic systems have transitioned from a democracy to an oligarchy, in which power is held by wealthy elites. We admire the ultra-rich as shining examples of the American Dream, but they've redefined the rules in their favor and shut out everyone else.

How Wealth was Won in the First Gilded Age

To be gilded refers to something being adorned or highlighted with gold, or anything of golden color. It has a beautiful or spectacular appearance that masks the fact that it is worthless.

The Gilded Age is the name given to the period in American history between the Civil War and the turn of the twentieth century when economic growth was rapid. It was characterized by several factors, including the rise of big business, the growth of cities, and the rise of a new class of millionaires.

The Gilded Age is credited with making America a wealthy and powerful nation, but it had a dark side. That is why American author and humorist Mark Twain called the late 19th century the *Gilded Age*. By this, he meant that the period was glittering on the surface but corrupt underneath. This was a period when greedy, corrupt industrialists, bankers, and politicians got very rich while the working class suffered.

It was wealthy tycoons who had the most political power during the Gilded Age, not politicians. By 1890, the richest 1% of Americans owned more than half of all wealth in the United States. Meanwhile, the richest

12% owned an astounding 86%. The rest of America was much poorer—the bottom 44% only had 1.2% of all wealth.

The Homestead Act

The Homestead Act, which allowed individuals to claim land in the western United States, was one of the most significant causes of the concentration of wealth during this era. This prompted a large movement of Americans to the West, where they could establish farms. The homesteaders were given 160 acres of land if they agreed to live on it and cultivate it for five years. The goal of the Homestead Act was to promote westward expansion and to increase the amount of farmland in America. However, it had the unintended consequence of concentrating wealth in the hands of a few. The reason for this is that many of the homesteaders were unable to successfully farm their land.

While 160 acres may have been sufficient for an eastern farmer, it was simply not enough to sustain agriculture on the dry plains, and scarce natural vegetation made raising livestock on the prairie difficult. As a result, in many areas, the original homesteader did not stay on the land long enough to fulfill the claim. They didn't have the money or the experience to do so. As a result, they were forced to sell their land to wealthy capitalists who did. This resulted in a concentration of wealth and power in the hands of a few. People who stuck it out and kept their homesteads were rewarded with new opportunities as transportation got easier.

Federal Indian policy also contributed to the accumulation of wealth during this period. The United States government forcibly removed Native Americans from their ancestral lands to make room for white settlers. This process, known as Indian removal, was devastating for Native American tribes. Many were forcibly relocated to reservations, where they were often unable to sustain themselves. The United States government also appropriated Native American land for various development projects, such as the building of the transcontinental railroad. This process led to the displacement of Native Americans and the concentration of their land in the hands of a few.

The Transcontinental Railroad

The Transcontinental Railroad was a major project that was completed during the Gilded Age. It connected the East and West coasts of the United States, making it easier for people and goods to travel between these regions. The completion of the railroad led to increased trade and commerce, which further enriched the already wealthy class of Americans. It spurred economic growth and led to the development of new cities, such as Omaha, Nebraska, and Salt Lake City, Utah.

The new railroads also provided relatively easy transportation for homesteaders, and new immigrants were lured westward by railroad companies eager to sell off once-public land at inflated prices. The Homestead Act and other land grants had already enticed settlers to move west, but the railroad made it much easier for them to do so. The railroad companies advertised the West as a land of opportunity, and many Americans were eager to take advantage of these opportunities. Consequently, the population of the American West grew rapidly during the late 19th century.

The Transcontinental Railroad project was made possible by the Homestead Act and several other state and federal land grants, including the Pacific Railway Acts of 1862 and 1864. These land grants allowed the railroad companies to build their tracks across public lands. The 1864 law also gave the railroad the mineral rights to their land as well, which were valuable because of the California Gold Rush.

The Union Pacific Railroad, which built the eastern portion of the transcontinental railroad, was the biggest beneficiary of these land grants. It received more than 8 million acres of land, worth an estimated $100 million. The company also received $27 million in government loans. This made Union Pacific one of the richest and most powerful corporations in America. Railroad barons such as Jay Gould and Cornelius Vanderbilt became some of the richest men in America.

The Growth of Cities

The Gilded Age ushered in the development of new cities and the growth of existing ones. This was largely due to the industrialization of America and the influx of immigrants. New York City, Chicago, Philadelphia, and Boston all experienced population growth during the late 19th century. New York City's population more than tripled, from 1 million in 1860 to 3.4 million in 1890. Chicago's population grew from 300,000 to 1.7 million during the same period. These cities became centers of commerce and industry, and they attracted people from all over the world.

Many of these new arrivals were poor immigrants who came in search of a better life. They often found themselves working in factories or sweatshops for long hours with little pay. Life in the cities was often difficult, and poverty was widespread. Crime rates were also high, and life was often dangerous. The growth of the cities led to the development of new social problems, such as overcrowding, crime, and poverty. Wealthy Americans were insulated from the harsh realities of life in the slums, but poor immigrants and working-class Americans were forced to endure these conditions. Despite the difficult conditions of life in the cities, many Americans continued to believe in the promise of the American Dream.

The Gilded Age saw the birth of many modern-day inventions. Urbanization and technological innovation paved the way for a slew of engineering breakthroughs, including bridges and canals, elevators and skyscrapers, trolley lines, and subways. The steel industry boomed, and steel-framed buildings became the norm in American cities. The telegraph and the telephone were invented, and the first transatlantic cable was laid. The phonograph and motion pictures were also introduced during this period.

These inventions changed the way Americans lived and worked, and they had a profound impact on American culture. The invention of electricity revolutionized home illumination and created an unrivaled, flourishing nightlife. Art and literature thrived, and the wealthy filled their palatial homes with valuable works of art and expensive decorations. These advances led to a more modern and efficient America, but they also created new monopolies and increased the gap between rich and poor. The wealthy class benefited immensely from the economic growth of the cities while the poor and working class saw little to no benefit.

The Rise of Big Business

The rise of big business was another factor that contributed to the concentration of wealth during the Gilded Age. The industrial revolution led to the development of new technologies and the growth of factories. This allowed businesses to produce more goods at a lower cost, which led to increased profits. A hands-off, laissez-faire capitalism was the prevailing economic philosophy of the time, which allowed businesses to operate without government interference. This led to a period of intense competition, as businesses fought for market share.

The government also favored business interests over those of the people. For example, the Homestead Act of 1862 gave free land to settlers who agreed to develop it. This Act led to the displacement of Native Americans and the development of large farms and ranches. The government also provided subsidies and loans to businesses, which helped them grow larger and more powerful. The size and power of these businesses increased, as did the gap between rich and poor. The owners of these businesses became very wealthy, while the workers who labored in the factories did not. Railroad tycoons, oil barons, and steel magnates were some of the most famous businessmen of the Gilded Age. The Sherman Anti-Trust Act of 1890 was supposed to curtail the power of monopolies, but it was poorly enforced and did little to stop the growth of big business.

A Period of Corruption

The Gilded Age was also a period of corruption. Industrialists and bankers bought off politicians to get what they wanted. They used their money to influence elections and pass laws that benefited them. This led to a government that was controlled by the wealthy, not the people. These men used union-busting, fraud, intimidation, violence, and their extensive political connections to gain an advantage over any competitors. They amassed enormous fortunes, and they used their wealth to further consolidate their power.

Some wealthy entrepreneurs, such as Andrew Carnegie, John D. Rockefeller, and Henry Frick, are often referred to as robber barons but they may not fit the mold exactly. Although they built huge monopolies, often by crushing any small business or competitor in their way, they were also generous philanthropists. They didn't always rely on political ploys to build their empires. A few of them attempted to improve the lives of their workers, donated millions to charity and nonprofit organizations, and supported their communities by providing funding for everything from libraries and hospitals to universities, public parks, and zoos. On the whole, however, the Gilded Age was a time when the rich got richer and the poor got poorer. The concentration of wealth led to increased social tensions, which would eventually erupt in the form of the Progressive movement.

The End of the Gilded Age

The Gilded Age came to an end with the Panic of 1893, which was a financial crisis that triggered an economic depression. This marked the beginning of a new era, known as the Progressive Era, which sought to address problems that had arisen during the Gilded Age and bring about social and economic reform. The Progressives advocated for the regulation of big business, the protection of workers, and the passage of landmark legislation, such as the Sherman Anti-Trust Act, the Federal Trade Commission Act, and the Pure Food and Drug Act. The income tax was also introduced during this time. The Progressive Era also saw the rise of labor unions, which gave workers more bargaining power. These reforms helped to curb the power of big business and level the playing field somewhat between the rich and the poor, but the concentration of wealth continued. The rich got richer and the poor got poorer, and this trend has continued in the United States up to the present day.

CHAPTER 5

For What It's Worth

The Rules of the Oligarchy Economy

For What It's Worth by Buffalo Springfield speaks to the power of standing up for what you believe in. Even after more than 50 years, it continues to be an anthem for those seeking change and justice in our world.

Although there are a few differences, the parallels between the Gilded Age and the present day are striking. During this period, extreme wealth imbalances, hyper-partisanship, virulent anti-immigrant prejudice, and heightened concern about money in politics became widespread. Union-busting, cheating, intimidation, and violence are all back in vogue. Using political connections to gain an edge is a common practice once again. Isn't it strange how similar things have happened?

How Wealth is Being Won in the Second Gilded Age

The Second Gilded Age is a term used to describe the current period of economic inequality and hyper-partisanship in the United States. This period, which began around 1990, has been defined by vast wealth inequality, political polarization, and growing concern about money in politics. It has been compared to the first Gilded Age of the late 19th and early 20th centuries due to its similarities in terms of income disparity and identity-based partisanship. The implications of this Second Gilded Age are far-reaching and have sparked debate on how best to address these issues.

The Rise of the Financial Industry

Personal, consumer, and corporate financial services are the three main categories of business in the financial industry. Personal finance includes services such as banking, insurance, investments, and retirement planning. Consumer finance encompasses credit, loans, and debt management. Corporate finance includes activities such as mergers and acquisitions, venture capital, and initial public offerings (*IPOs*).

The financial industry has grown rapidly in recent decades, and it now accounts for a significant portion of the economy. In 1970, the financial industry made up about 2.5% of the economy. By 2016, it had grown to 8.5%. This means that the financial industry now makes up a larger share of the economy than it did in the Gilded Age and its profits are increasingly going to the top 1%. In 2016, the top 1% of financial workers made an average of $2.7 million, which is more than double what they made in 1980.

In the 1980s, there was a deregulation of the financial industry, making it easier for banks and other financial institutions to engage in risky behavior. This deregulation has led to increased instability in the financial system and has contributed to the 2008 economic crisis. In the 1990s, the industry lobbied for the repeal of the Glass-Steagall Act, which had been enacted during the Great Depression to separate commercial banks from investment banks.

The repeal of this law led to the creation of *too big to fail* banks, which are so large and interconnected that their failure would cause a financial crisis. The crisis led to the bailouts of several large banks, which were deemed *too big to fail*. The bailouts cost taxpayers billions of dollars and contributed to the growth of the national debt.

The financial industry has also been a major source of campaign contributions to politicians and has used its power and influence to get favorable treatment from the government. The industry has benefited from bailouts, tax breaks, and deregulation. The result is an economy that is increasingly rigged in favor of the wealthy and powerful.

The Privatization of Public Services

In the past, public services such as education and healthcare were provided by the government, which means that these services were paid for through taxes and were available to everyone. In recent years, there has been a trend toward the privatization of public services, which means that private companies are now providing these services. Typically, these businesses are for-profit and make money by charging consumers for their goods or services. This has led to a two-tier system in which the wealthy can afford to pay for private services while the poor are left with lower-quality public services.

The privatization of public services has been a boon for the companies that provide these services, but it has been a disaster for the people who use them. Privatization has led to the deterioration of public services because private companies are motivated by profit, not by providing a service to the public, and often cut corners and provide lower-quality services. The privatization of public services also has led to the growth of for-profit prisons, which are motivated by profit rather than by providing rehabilitation or reform. This has led to an increase in the number of people in prison, as well as to widespread abuse and mistreatment of prisoners. Consequently, most people believe that privatization is bad for the economy and bad for society.

The Growth of CEO Pay

Corporate Chief Executive Officer (*CEO*) compensation has increased dramatically in recent years. In the 1950s, CEOs made about 20 times the average worker's salary. By the 1990s, they were making about 100 times the average worker's salary. And, by 2016, they were making an average of 271 times the average worker's salary. This trend is a result of the growing power of CEOs and the decline of unions. Unions used to provide a countervailing force to the power of corporations, but their power has declined in recent years. As a result, corporations have been able to increase CEO compensation without any checks or balances. This trend has contributed to the growing inequality in the United States, as the rich have gotten richer while the middle class has stagnated.

The high level of CEO compensation is due to several factors, including the deregulation of the financial industry, the trend toward privatization of public services, and the growth of CEO pay relative to worker pay. It is often justified by the argument that CEOs are paid for their performance. However, a study by economists at the University of California, Berkeley found that CEO pay is not correlated with company performance. In other words, CEOs are not paid more because they do a better job, but because they have the power to negotiate higher pay for themselves. This is why many people believe that CEO pay is excessive and contributes to income inequality.

The Growth of Tax Incentives

To attract businesses, produce jobs, and stimulate economic growth, many American cities and states offer financial incentives in the form of tax breaks, loans, and other subsidies. Big tech companies and other businesses have avoided paying billions of dollars in taxes thanks to the growth of tax breaks and loopholes. For example, Amazon paid no federal income taxes in 2017 or 2018 on profits of $11 billion. Meanwhile, small businesses and middle-class families are shouldering a larger share of the tax burden.

The use of tax incentives to attract businesses is a controversial practice. Studies have found that the vast majority of the benefits from these tax breaks go to shareholders and executives, not to workers. Critics argue that it is a form of corporate welfare that benefits wealthy businesses and CEOs at the expense of taxpayers. They also argue that these incentives are often ineffective and a waste of money. Proponents of tax incentives argue that they are necessary to compete for businesses in the global economy. They also argue that these incentives can create jobs and stimulate economic growth.

The use of tax incentives is likely to continue to grow in the United States, as cities and states compete for businesses. This competition can lead to a race to the bottom, as cities and states offer businesses more and more generous tax breaks. This can result in less money for the city or state, and this can lead to cuts in public services. The growth of tax incentives has thus contributed to the decline of the public sector and the growth of income inequality. Instead of providing incentives to businesses that have an actual or potential negative impact on our shared environment and community, a better way to create jobs and spur economic growth would be to invest in public goods and services, education, local job skills, land development, and infrastructure. All of these have a greater return on investment for local economies.

The Rise of Dark Money

Previously, wealthy individuals and corporations could only influence politics by donating to campaigns, and this was a more transparent process. But today, we have something called dark money, which is money that is spent on political activities without the requirement that the donors be identified. This allows special interests to buy influence without being held accountable by the public.

In 2010, the Supreme Court issued a ruling in the Citizens United case that allowed corporations and unions to spend unlimited amounts of money to influence elections. This ruling opened the floodgates for dark money in politics. Since then, dark money groups have spent about $1 billion on ads and mailers to try to influence elections. This has created a situation in which a small number of wealthy people have an outsized influence on our government.

Citizens who are inundated with political advertising paid for by anonymous contributors may be unable to evaluate the legitimacy and possible motives of the wealthy corporate or individual sponsors behind those messages. As a result, dark money has the potential to distort our democracy and create an oligarchy in which a small number of wealthy people have an outsized influence on our government.

In 2012, the IRS launched an investigation into whether dark money groups were violating their tax-exempt status by engaging in political activity. However, the investigation was hampered by a lack of transparency and was ultimately dropped. As a result, dark money groups are now able to operate with little oversight.

Control of the Media

A small number of individuals and corporations now control the majority of the media. This concentration of media ownership allows these individuals and corporations to shape public opinion to further their interests. It also can lead to a situation in which the public is only exposed to one side of the story. This can make it difficult for people to make informed decisions about the issues that affect their lives.

Facebook and Google are also major players in the media landscape. Together, they control about 60% of the digital advertising market. This gives them a lot of power to determine what news people see. In 2016, Facebook was accused of allowing fake news to proliferate on its platform. This fake news had the potential to influence the outcome of the presidential election. As a result, Facebook has come under pressure to crack down on fake news. However, it is not clear how effective these efforts have been.

How the Ultra-Rich Maintain Power and Wealth in an Oligarchy Economy

One of the most common ways that the ultra-rich maintain their power and wealth is by rigging the rules of the oligarchy economy in their favor. This can take many forms, but some of the most common are listed below.

- They use their political clout to get laws and regulations passed that favor their businesses.

- They use their economic power to drive down wages, benefits, and working conditions.

- They use their financial resources to buy up small businesses, driving up prices and putting people out of work.

- They use their media resources to control the narrative and shape public opinion in their favor.

- They use their philanthropic resources to buy influence and create a positive public image for themselves.

- They use private school education to groom the next generation and gain preferential access to education, jobs, and other opportunities.

- They use intergenerational wealth transfer mechanisms to create a self-perpetuating cycle of privilege that is passed down from generation to generation.

Political Power

The present age is one in which political populism has taken center stage. However, it's not the same as the populist democratic movement that followed the last Gilded Age, which fought to curb corruption and protect people's rights while also increasing the power of ordinary citizens. The contemporary populism movement is connected with a style of government that is authoritarian—a type of government in which one person has a lot of power.

Populist authoritarian movements are led by charismatic leaders who appeal to and claim to embody the will of the people. They do this to consolidate their power. In this personalized form of politics, political parties lose their significance, and elections confirm the leader's power rather than reflect the various allegiances of the people. Extreme nationalism, racism, conspiracy theories, and scapegoating of despised minorities are hallmarks of some forms of authoritarian populism. Each of these methods is intended to strengthen the leader's power, divert public attention away from failures, and disguise the nature of the leader's rule or the true causes of economic or social issues from the people.

Oligarchs use their political clout to get laws and regulations passed that favor their businesses. Specific examples of this include laws that lower taxes on the wealthy, weaken environmental regulations, and loosen financial regulations. In 2017, for instance, the ultra-rich used their political clout to get a huge tax cut passed that favored them and their businesses. The top 1% of earners got an average tax cut of $50,000, while the bottom 99% got an average tax cut of $460. This was accomplished by lobbying congress and making campaign donations to lawmakers.

The Tax Cuts and Jobs Act of 2017 had a good-sounding name, but it was essentially a politically-motivated ruse. It was ushered in and carried out by a self-proclaimed billionaire and his accomplices, using language that was intended to appeal to average people. It has been widely criticized by tax experts as a poorly-designed and unfair law that benefits the ultra-rich at the expense of everyone else.

The subprime mortgage crisis of 2007-2008 was caused in part by the deregulation of the financial industry. This was accomplished by a concerted effort on the part of oligarchs and their political allies to weaken or eliminate laws and regulations that had been put in place to protect consumers and prevent another Great Depression. The deregulation of the financial industry led to widespread fraud, corruption, and abuse, which ultimately resulted in the loss of trillions of dollars of wealth and the displacement of millions of people.

The oligarchs who caused the crisis walked away with billions of dollars while average Americans were left to deal with the consequences. In 2008, Congress passed a law that bailed out the financial industry to the tune of $700 billion. This was done to prevent the collapse of the economy, but it was also a way to ensure that the people who caused the crisis didn't suffer any consequences for their actions.

In 2010, the Supreme Court handed down a decision in the Citizens United case that allowed corporations and wealthy individuals to spend unlimited amounts of money to influence elections. This had a profound impact on American politics, as it essentially allowed the rich to buy elections. In the 2012 election, for example, outside spending by corporations and wealthy individuals totaled $6 billion. This was more than double the amount spent in the 2008 election. The vast majority of this money went to support Republican candidates. The Citizens United decision has been a boon for oligarchs, as it has allowed them to use their money to buy elections and gain more political power. It has also had a deleterious effect on democracy, as it has made it harder for average citizens to have a say in the political process.

The supreme court, which once was considered a nonpartisan institution, has become increasingly politicized in recent years. This is due in large part to the fact that the court has been stacked with conservative appointees, all of whom were nominated by Republican presidents who did not achieve victory in the popular vote but rather via an antiquated and undemocratic Electoral College. The court has grown more activist in recent years, and it has handed down several judgments that have benefited the wealthy and powerful. In the summer of 2022, the court ended 50 years of federal abortion rights, expanded gun rights, weakened the power of the Environmental Protection Agency, and appeared to be on track to undermine contraception access, same-sex relationships, and same-sex marriage.

In addition to using their political clout to get laws passed, oligarchs also use it to block laws that would benefit the average person. One example of this is the minimum wage. The federal minimum wage has been stuck at $7.25 an hour for over a decade, even though the cost of living has gone up significantly during that time. This has been a huge windfall for corporations, who have been able to pocket the difference between what their workers are paid and what it costs to live on. Other measures that would have benefited the middle class have been cut short, including rules that would have made it easier for employees to organize and laws that would have closed the loopholes that allow businesses to avoid taxes.

Oligarchs have also used their political clout to weaken environmental regulations. This has allowed them to pollute the air and water without consequence, and it has put the health of average people at risk. In some cases, oligarchs have even been able to get environmental regulations repealed outright. One notable example is the Clean Power Plan, which was a set of Obama-era regulations designed to reduce greenhouse gas emissions from power plants.

President Obama's successor worked to repeal the Clean Power Plan, which would have been a huge victory for oligarchs, as it would have allowed them to pollute with impunity. On the last day of the 45th president's term, the second-highest court in the land struck down one of the most damaging anti-environmental actions of his administration. During the same period, however, more than 35 million acres of public land were lost or threatened with loss of protection, amounting to roughly the area of Florida. After a uranium company lobbied the government, Bears Ears National Monument was reduced by 85% in December 2017. Andrew Wheeler, who served as the 15th administrator of the United States Environmental Protection Agency (*EPA*) from 2019 to 2021, was a big part of this effort.

These are just a few of the political ploys enacted in a previous administration that, at times, appeared to be designed specifically to dismantle any progress that had been made toward a more just and equitable society.

Economic Power

The economic power of the present-day ultra-rich is unparalleled in our history. The level of economic inequality is even higher than it was during the Gilded Age when the top 1% of the U.S. population owned 51% of all wealth. The concentration of wealth in the hands of the few has had several harmful effects on our economy. It has led to a decrease in consumer spending, as the majority of people do not have disposable income to purchase goods and services. This has been a major drag on economic growth, as consumer spending accounts for 70% of all economic activity.

Another effect of the concentration of wealth is that it has made our economy less stable. When the rich have a larger share of the pie, they are more likely to save their money rather than invest it in productive enterprises. In recent years, the increase in cash held by U.S. enterprises has been dramatic, exploding from $1.6 trillion in 2000 to roughly $5.8 trillion today. This trend has worried investors, who would want the money either invested or paid out as dividends rather than kept idle. This leads to a decrease in investment and an increase in economic inequality.

Some economists have argued that the concentration of wealth is not necessarily a bad thing, as it can lead to more investment and economic growth. However, the evidence does not support this claim. In reality, the concentration of wealth is a drag on economic growth and stability, and it gives the rich too much political power.

One of the most popular policies promoted by the government in recent decades, and which is still fiercely defended, is *trickle-down economics*. The trickle-down economics theory is the idea that when businesses, high-income earners, and people who own a lot of assets get tax cuts, the benefits will *trickle-down* to everyone else. Trickle-down economics holds that the Reagan and Bush tax cuts should have benefited everyone. The exact opposite occurred, as income disparity worsened. After-tax household income rose 6% for the bottom fifth between 1979 and 2005. That might appear to be good news until you compare it with what happened to the top fifth. Their income shot up by 80%. The top 1% increased their income by three times. It appears that prosperity has been trickling up instead of trickling down.

Now, there is increasing talk among political *conservatives* about cutting Social Security payments and Medicare reimbursements—programs that are vital to the economic security of millions of Americans. Calling these programs *entitlements*, as if they are some kind of handout instead of earned benefits that workers have been paying into for decades, they want to reduce or eliminate them. In reality, it's a cynical ploy to get rid of programs that have helped millions of Americans and a way to further increase the concentration of wealth and power in our society.

Working conditions have fared no better during this second Gilded Age. Although we have some protections that were put in place following the first Gilded Age, such as the 8-hour workday, the 40-hour workweek, and occupational safety regulations, these have all been under attack in recent years. The right to unionize has been under assault, as companies use their power to keep workers from organizing. Many workers are now classified as *independent contractors*, which means they do not have the same protections as employees. This has led to a decline in wages and a decrease in benefits, such as healthcare and retirement savings.

Financial Control

A monopoly is when one company has a lot of control over an industry or sector, to the point where no other companies can compete. A few monopolies could be considered beneficial, such as electrical utilities or water providers, which are essential services that need to be delivered efficiently. However, most monopolies stifle competition and allow companies to charge higher prices and rake in huge profits. There are four main types of monopolies:

- Natural monopolies, where one company can provide a service more cheaply than any other company because of economies of scale.

- Technological monopolies, where a company has a patent or copyright on a product or service.

- Government-sanctioned monopolies, where the government grants a company the exclusive right to provide a service, such as the U.S. Postal Service.

- Market share monopolies, where one company has such a large share of the market that it can effectively set prices.

Monopolies create many problems for both the society and economy. When a monopoly exists, there is little incentive for the company to innovate or improve its products or services. The problem of monopolies is compounded by the fact that many of these corporations are now global in scope. This gives them even more power, as they can operate in countries with weak regulatory regimes and take advantage of workers there who have no protections. They can also use their financial resources to influence politicians and get favorable laws passed. This increases their power and allows them to further rig the system in their favor. Remember the concept of *too big to fail* from the 2008 financial crisis? That's what happens when a monopoly gets too big and powerful. The government is forced to bail them out because they are essential to the economy, but this just makes the problem worse.

Oligarchs use their financial resources to buy up small businesses, driving up prices and putting people out of work. While we have anti-trust laws on the books to guard against monopolistic practices, the reality is that a handful of corporations now control vast sectors of the economy, from food production to healthcare to banking. This gives them an immense amount of power over our lives. And because these corporations are often global in scope, they are beyond the reach of any one government. This makes it very difficult to regulate them or hold them accountable for their actions.

Media Control

Oligarchs use their media platforms to dominate the conversation and shape public opinion in their favor. In the United States, six businesses (*Comcast, Disney, Time Warner, Fox, CBS, and Viacom*) dominate almost 90% of media organizations. The Murdoch family, which controls the News Corporation (*the operator of Fox News*), has media and publishing branches on five different continents. News Corp. is notorious for practicing predatory capitalism in the news industry, which jeopardizes media diversity and democracy.

Broadcast and cable news outlets are not the only targets of media control. Social media platforms, such as Facebook and Twitter, are also increasingly dominated by a few large corporations. Eighty-three percent of all internet traffic is controlled by just four companies *(Google, Amazon, Facebook, and Apple)*. This gives these companies immense power to shape the online conversation and control what information we have access to.

Tesla billionaire Elon Musk's acquisition of the social media platform Twitter has rightly drawn concern from critics. They worry that he will have too much control over the news media. But this is not just about free speech, as Musk would like to frame it. It is also about the quest by billionaires to control the news media. His goals are similar to those of Jeff Bezos, who owns the Washington Post, Rupert Murdoch, who owns Fox networks and several newspapers, and the descendants of Sinclair Broadcast Group, Inc. *(SBG)* founder Julian Sinclair Smith, the owner and operator of the most local TV stations in the nation—to shape public opinion around their world views. The problem with media consolidation is that it gives too much power to a small number of people. It allows them to control the flow of information and shape public opinion to their benefit. This is a dangerous situation for any democracy.

The U.S. population is more polarized than ever, and the media is partly to blame. At an annual media and communications conference in 2022, Sinclair CEO Chris Ripley told his audience that a politically divided America is *very good for our business*. His company's local TV operation has a reputation for highly partisan commentaries and has required all of its affiliates to air *must-run* segments that were often criticized as biased and misleading. Ripley isn't the only media executive to see divisions in society as a business opportunity. Rupert Murdoch, the chairman and CEO of Fox Corporation, said in 2006 that *the more divided the world gets, the better it is for us*. Rupert has shown that it's relatively easy to *stir up the lizard brain* and cash in on fear in society.

The fairness doctrine was a policy of the United States Federal Communications Commission *(FCC)*, introduced in 1949, that required the holders of broadcast licenses both to present controversial issues of public importance and to do so in a manner that was, in the Commission's view, honest, equitable and balanced. The doctrine was rescinded by the FCC in 1987. The repeal of the fairness doctrine enabled the rise of divisive and vicious messaging and *news* based on ideology and opinion rather than facts. The devastating truth is that the majority of us who live in the middle-class share many of the same ideals and objectives. But, we are continually duped by wealthy people with warped viewpoints and political motives into fighting one another.

Philanthropic Influence

It's no secret that the wealthy have more influence than the average person. But, what is less well known is the extent to which they use their influence to protect their wealth and privilege and further their interests. The truth is that the wealthy have a disproportionate amount of power to use their philanthropic resources to buy influence and create a positive public image for themselves. For example, the family of David and Charles Koch, commonly referred to as the Koch brothers, have a combined net worth is $100 billion, which is good enough to make them the second wealthiest family in America.

The family is also extremely influential in politics, especially in far-right-wing issues, and has been patiently reshaping the Republican Party and conservatism in America since at least the 1970s. The Koch brothers have donated millions of dollars to higher education institutions. In return, these institutions have given the brothers a platform to disseminate their political ideology and advance their business interests. The Koch brothers have also used their philanthropy to support conservative think tanks and policy organizations. These organizations help to shape public opinion and promote the brothers' political and economic agenda.

These days, when wealthy individuals make large donations, they are celebrated as heroes. It was not always this way. John D. Rockefeller's proposal for the establishment of the Rockefeller Foundation in 1909 met with fierce resistance. The notion was initially criticized by Former President Teddy Roosevelt and then-President William Taft, with Roosevelt declaring, *No amount of charities in spending such fortunes can compensate in any way for the misconduct in acquiring them.*

The lack of transparency and potential conflicts of interest inherent in most large-scale charity efforts are a major concern for democratic governments and customs. We should be more critical and skeptical of rich people giving away their money. It is often done with ulterior motives and can harm society. The charitable contribution tax deduction benefits the wealthy more than the middle-class or poor people. When rich individuals give to charity, they get a larger sum of money back from the government than do middle-class and impoverished people.

Private Schools

From an early age, children of the ultra-rich are groomed to take their place in the American oligarchy. They attend private schools, which are often segregated by race and class. At these schools, the children of the wealthy are socialized with other members of their class and learn how to maintain and reproduce their privileged position in society. Relationships formed in these environments often last a lifetime and help to solidify the power of the American oligarchy. Variations of the *old-boy network* can be found in all walks of American life, but it is especially pronounced among the ultra-rich. These cliques provide their members with preferential access to education, jobs, and other opportunities.

While the children of the wealthy attend private schools, the children of the working and middle class are increasingly attending underfunded public schools. In many cases, these public schools are overcrowded, understaffed, and lack the resources to provide quality education. As a result, the children of the rich are getting an even better education than they would have in the past, while the children of the poor are falling further behind. This increased educational inequality is one of the factors that is widening the gap between the rich and everyone else in America.

Intergenerational Transfers

The American oligarchy is also perpetuated by intergenerational transfers of wealth. This concentration of wealth is made possible, in part, by the fact that wealthy Americans can pass their money down to their children. In addition to receiving a sizable inheritance, the children of the rich also benefit from their parents' connections and social capital. These advantages give them a leg up in the job market and make it more likely that they will become wealthy themselves. The result is a self-perpetuating cycle of privilege that is passed down from generation to generation. In short, the American oligarchy is perpetuated by the intergenerational transfer of wealth. The ultra-rich can pass their money down to their children, who then use it to get a leg up in life. This creates a cycle of inequality that is difficult to break.

The family office is one financial structure that allows the ultra-rich to keep their wealth in the family. A family office is a private wealth management firm that provides financial and legal services to a single family. These firms often have teams of accountants, investment managers, and lawyers who work to grow and protect the family's wealth. While the use of family offices is not new, they have become more popular in recent years as the wealthy seek to avoid taxes and protect their assets from creditors. One study found that the number of family offices in the United States increased by 50 percent between 2010 and 2015.

Trust funds and family foundations are other structures that are used to maintain control of the family's wealth and pass it down through the generations. The benefits of trusts and foundations are not just available to the ultra-rich; however, they are more likely to be used by wealthy families because of the high cost of setting them up and the expert advice that is needed to manage them. But, the tax advantages and asset protection they provide make them an attractive option for the ultra-rich.

Another form of wealth transfer is real estate, which can appreciate over time and provide a source of income for future generations. Real property may take the form of a family home, a vacation property, or a commercial building. Whatever the form, real estate is often used as a way to transfer wealth from one generation to the next.

Non-traditional assets like collectibles and precious metals are some of the tools many wealthy families use. The art market has seen a boom in recent years, with prices for some pieces reaching hundreds of millions of dollars. Collectibles and precious metals can also serve as a store of value and a hedge against inflation. For the ultra-rich, these assets are often seen as a way to diversify their portfolios and protect their wealth.

CHAPTER 6

The Times They Are A-Changin'

The Economic Trends Favoring Those at the Top

The Times They Are A-Changin' by Bob Dylan resonates even today, as it speaks to the power of collective action in bringing about meaningful change. It is a reminder that we all have a responsibility to fight for justice and equality, no matter how daunting the task may seem.

The American economy has changed in ways that favor those at the top. The decline of the middle class and the rise of inequality are two of the most significant changes. Globalization, the decline of unions, changes in the tax code, deregulation, the Great Recession, and the COVID-19 pandemic have only exacerbated these trends. As a result, the middle class is struggling while the rich are getting richer. This is not sustainable and will eventually lead to an economic collapse. To build community wealth, we need to level the playing field and create opportunities for everyone to participate. We need to ensure that everyone has a voice in decision-making and that the resources of our community are used for the benefit of all.

7 Economic Trends are Favoring Those at the Top

The American economy has changed in ways that favor those at the top. In the past, most Americans worked in manufacturing or agriculture. This meant that there were many opportunities for individuals to get good-paying jobs without a college degree. But today, these jobs have been replaced by service sector jobs that are often low-paying and provide few benefits. The economy today is based on knowledge and information technology. This means that individuals with college degrees and specialized skills are more likely to succeed, while those without a college degree or specialized skills are at a disadvantage.

In the past, when the economy grew, everyone benefited. Today, however, most of the benefits from economic growth are going to those at the top. This is due to several factors, including globalization, the decline of unions, changes in the tax code, deregulation, and the rise of new industries like tech and finance. Other events, including the Great Recession and the COVID-19 pandemic, disproportionately harmed those at the bottom, while those at the top continued to prosper.

1) Globalization

Globalization is the process of expanding economic ties between countries. This has led to a more interconnected world, where goods, services, people, and money can move more easily than ever before. The North American Free Trade Agreement (*NAFTA*) is an example of globalization. NAFTA is a trade agreement between the United States, Mexico, and Canada that removed barriers to trade and investment. The goal of NAFTA was to promote economic growth by making it easier for businesses to operate in North America.

The rise of globalization has had a mixed impact on the American economy. On the one hand, it has created new opportunities for businesses and workers. For example, it's now easier for companies to set up operations in other countries, and this can lead to new jobs for American workers. On the other hand, globalization has also led to job losses as companies move their operations to other countries where labor is cheaper. In addition, globalization has put downward pressure on wages, as workers in other countries are willing to work for less money.

2) The Decline of Unions

Unions are organizations that represent workers and bargain with employers for better wages and working conditions. They help to ensure that workers receive a fair share of the profits they help to generate. In the past, unions were a major force in the American economy. They helped to raise wages and improve working conditions for all workers, not just union members. However, in recent years, unions have declined in both membership and power. In 1970, there were roughly 17 million union members in the United States, or over 30% of private-sector employees. By 2002, it had declined by more than half. In 2014, there were just over 14 million union members in the United States, or around 11% of private-sector employees. The decline of unions has been especially pronounced in the private sector, where only 7% of workers are unionized. In the public sector, however, unions are still fairly strong, with 35% of workers being unionized.

The decline of unions has hurt workers, who have lost a powerful advocate for their interests, and it has had a significant impact on the American economy. In addition, the decline of unions has contributed to the growth of income inequality, as union workers have seen their wages stagnate while those at the top have continued to prosper. There are several reasons for the decline of unions, including globalization and the decline of manufacturing. In addition, changes in the economy and the law have made it harder for unions to organize new members. Large companies have also become more resistant to unionization for various reasons, including the desire to keep costs low and the belief that unions make it harder to be agile and respond to change. In reality, large companies favor the status quo, and unions are often a force for change. The bottom line is that the decline of unions has made it harder for workers to get ahead, and it's one of the reasons why income inequality has grown in recent years.

3) Changes in the Tax Code

The tax code is the set of laws that govern how taxes are collected and spent. In recent years, there have been several changes to the tax code that have favored those at the top. The last law to change rates was the Tax Cuts and Jobs Act of 2017. The primary features of this law were a reduction in the corporate tax rate from 35 percent to 21 percent and a reduction in the top marginal income tax rate, which is the rate of tax paid beyond a certain threshold. In the United States, the top marginal tax rate in 2020 was 37%. In the 1970s, the marginal tax rate for the top income brackets was 70%, which means that those at the top were paying a much higher rate than they are today. These changes have been criticized by some as being unfair to middle- and low-income taxpayers, as they receive a smaller tax cut than those at the top. In addition, the estate tax, which is a tax on inherited wealth, has been reduced. This benefits wealthy families who can pass their money down to future generations without paying taxes on it.

For the middle class, the effects of tax reform have been mixed. The Tax Cuts and Jobs Act did result in a tax cut for most middle-class families, but the size of the tax cut was smaller than for those in the top income brackets. In addition, the tax code changes have added to the national debt, which will likely have to be paid for by future generations through higher taxes. The changes to the tax code have been criticized for making income inequality worse. This is because the changes provide the most benefit to those who are already wealthy. In addition to changes in marginal tax rates, the tax code has become increasingly complex, making it more difficult for average Americans to understand and comply with the law. The primary reasons for these kinds of tax reforms are to lower taxes on businesses and the wealthy, which proponents argue will lead to economic growth. However, there is little evidence that tax cuts for the wealthy lead to economic growth, and they often result in increased budget deficits.

4) Deregulation

Deregulation is the process of removing or reducing government regulations. This can include regulations related to labor, the environment, and financial institutions. Deregulation can be beneficial for businesses, as it can make it easier to operate and expand. However, deregulation can also lead to negative consequences, such as increased pollution and financial instability. For the middle class, deregulation can lead to job loss and wage stagnation, as businesses seek to reduce costs. For example, the deregulation of the trucking industry in the 1980s led to a decline in wages for truck drivers.

Other deregulated industries, such as the airline and banking industries, have also seen wage stagnation or decline.

Deregulation can lead to increased income inequality, as those at the top are more likely to benefit from it. The biggest beneficiaries of deregulation are often large corporations and the wealthy, as they have the resources to take advantage of the new opportunities it provides. For example, the deregulation of the banking industry in the 1990s led to the creation of large banks that were *too big to fail*. These banks took on more risk, knowing that they would be bailed out by the government if they failed. This eventually led to the financial crisis of 2008, which had a devastating effect on the middle class. The environmental impacts of deregulation can also be severe. For example, the deregulation of the coal industry has led to increased air pollution and a decline in the quality of life for those living in coal-mining communities. Again, the biggest beneficiaries of deregulation are often the largest corporations, as they can externalize the costs of pollution onto society.

5) The Rise of New Industries

The rise of new industries like tech and finance has favored those with college degrees and specialized skills. These industries are often located in cities, which means that workers who live in rural areas are at a disadvantage. In addition, these industries tend to pay higher salaries than manufacturing, which has led to a widening of the income gap. The most rapid growth of tech and finance industry jobs occurred from the year 2000 to the year 2016. It was also during this period that the income gap between the top 1% and the rest of the population reached its highest level since the 1920s. At the same time that new industries were emerging, existing industries were in decline. This was particularly true of manufacturing, which lost millions of jobs from the year 2000 to the year 2016. The loss of manufacturing jobs has had a devastating effect on communities that relied on these jobs for their economic stability.

The rise of new industries and the decline of old industries has led to a change in the composition of the middle class. In the past, the middle class was largely made up of workers in manufacturing and other traditional industries. Today, the middle class is increasingly made up of workers in service industries, such as healthcare and education. This shift has made the middle class more vulnerable to economic downturns, as service jobs are often more susceptible to job loss than manufacturing jobs. The change in the composition of the middle class has also made it more difficult for families to achieve economic stability. In the past, a single breadwinner in a manufacturing job could support a family. Today, families often need two incomes to make ends meet. This is particularly true in high-cost areas, such as major cities. For example, the median rent for a two-bedroom apartment in San Francisco is $4,500 per month. This is an unaffordable amount for many families, particularly those who are living paycheck to paycheck.

6) *The Great Recession*

The Great Recession was a period of economic decline that began in 2007 and lasted for several years. The recession was caused by several factors, including the housing market crash, high levels of debt, and the failure of financial institutions. The recession led to job losses, wage cuts, and increases in poverty and inequality. The Great Recession had a particularly negative impact on middle-class families, as many lost their homes and savings. In addition, the recession contributed to the growth of income inequality, as those at the top were able to weather the economic downturn better than those at the bottom. The U.S. gross domestic product, which is a measure of the country's economic output, declined by 4.3% from the year 2007 to the year 2009. This was the sharpest decline since the Great Depression. The unemployment rate more than doubled, from less than 5 percent to 10 percent. It remained above 9% for the next two years. In total, 8.7 million jobs were lost during the Great Recession. It was also the longest recession, lasting eighteen months.

While the economy has recovered since the Great Recession, many middle-class families have not. This is due in part to the fact that many jobs that were lost during the recession, such as manufacturing jobs, have not returned. In addition, wages have failed to keep up with inflation, meaning that families' purchasing power has declined. As a result, many middle-class families are struggling to make ends meet. Inequality has also continued to grow in the years since the recession, as those at the top have seen their incomes rise while those at the bottom have seen their incomes stagnate or decline.

7) The COVID-19 Pandemic

The COVID-19 virus has caused widespread job losses, business closures, and economic decline. This was mainly because businesses were forced to shut down due to government-mandated social distancing measures. The pandemic has had a particularly negative impact on service industries, such as hospitality and tourism, which have been hit hard by the closures. In addition, the pandemic has led to a decrease in consumer spending, as many people are hesitant to spend money during such uncertain times. The COVID-19 pandemic has also exacerbated existing inequalities, as those who are already struggling financially have been hit the hardest by the economic downturn. The ultra-rich were not only able to withstand the economic consequences of lockdowns and uncertainty, but they also profited from them. During the epidemic, the world's billionaires' net worth increased by $3.9 trillion while the overall economy shrank by 3.7%.

The pandemic has also hurt the middle class by causing a decrease in home values. This is because many people are unable to make their mortgage payments or keep up with their property taxes. As a result, foreclosures and evictions are on the rise. This is likely to have a long-term impact on the middle class, as it will make it more difficult for families to accumulate wealth and attain economic stability. The pandemic has also led to an increase in government debt. This is because the government has had to spend trillions of dollars to bail out businesses and provide relief to families who have been impacted by the pandemic. The increase in government debt is likely to have negative consequences for the economy in the long run, as it will lead to higher taxes and inflation.

Supply chain issues caused by the pandemic have also led to inflation, as businesses have had to raise prices to cover their increased costs. This has been particularly difficult for middle-class families, as they have been struggling to make ends meet even before the pandemic. The combination of job losses, wage stagnation, and inflation has caused many middle-class families to fall into poverty. The pandemic is likely to cause an increase in poverty rates in the United States. This is because poverty is not just about having a low income, but about not having enough resources to meet basic needs. The pandemic has caused a decrease in resources, as well as an increase in needs. For example, families who can no longer afford to pay for child care or health care are more likely to fall into poverty.

7 Economic Trends May Lead to Greater Wealth Inequality

The economy is changing faster than ever before and this is expected to continue in the years to come. This will be driven by technological advancements, global competition, and demographic shifts. As the economy changes, so do the opportunities and challenges for businesses and workers. Those who have the greatest foresight and resources will be best positioned to take advantage of the changes and prosper. People who can't adapt will have a harder time succeeding than those who have more money to start with. This is sure to lead to greater inequality in the future. The following are some of the anticipated changes in the economy in the coming years:

1) The Aging of the Population

In 2040, about one in five Americans will be age 65 or older. That's more than twice as many people as in 2000. The aging of baby boomers means that older people are projected to be more numerous than children for the first time in U.S. history. In 2020, there were 3.5 working-age adults for every retirement-age person. By 2060, that ratio will drop to just 2.5 because fewer people will be in the workforce relative to the number of retirees. This trend is expected to have several consequences, including a shortage of workers, increased pressure on Social Security and Medicare, and a decline in the housing market.

In addition, the older population will require more health care, which could lead to higher insurance premiums and medical costs. Already, the cost of health care is one of the biggest drivers of inequality. The rich can afford better health care, which gives them an advantage in longevity and quality of life. The poor, on the other hand, often have to choose between food and medicine, which can lead to poor health and shorter lifespans. The home-care market in the U.S. is expected to grow from $100 billion in 2016 to $225 billion by 2024 as more baby boomers age and require assistance, but prefer to age in place. This is likely to create opportunities for businesses that provide in-home care services. The existing caregiver shortage is expected to worsen as the population ages, which could lead to higher wages for caregivers.

Some of these difficulties may be alleviated by the digital health technologies that are developing. Telehealth, for example, could allow doctors to remotely monitor patients and provide care at a lower cost. Remote patient monitoring is a digital health technology that is used to collect data from patients who are at home and provide it to their care team. This information can be used to improve the quality of care, prevent complications, and lower costs. Voice assistants, such as Amazon's Echo and Google Home, are also being used to provide health information and reminders, as well as to summon emergency services. These technologies are likely to become more prevalent in the coming years and could help to offset some of the challenges posed by an aging population.

2) The Rise of New Technologies

New technologies could lead to changes in the way we live and work. For example, self-driving cars could reduce the need for car ownership, and 3D printing could change the way we manufacture goods. These changes could lead to job losses in certain industries, as well as new opportunities in others. As a result of automation and digital advancements, labor demand is shifting away from basic low- to middle-level abilities to more advanced analytical, technical, and creative abilities. This has increased the premium on higher levels of education and skills.

The increased demand for higher-level skills is likely to lead to greater inequality, as those who have the necessary skills will be able to command higher wages, while those without will find it increasingly difficult to compete for jobs. On the supply side, however, providing employees with skills that go hand-in-hand with new technologies has been a major barrier to their wider adoption. There is a need for reskilling programs that can help workers transition to new industries and occupations. Education and training have been losing the race with technology.

The future of smart technologies may be bright. As much as two-thirds of potential productivity growth in the world's major economies over the next decade could come from the application of digital technologies.

But technological change is inherently disruptive and entails difficult transitions. With Intelligent policies, we could see stronger and more inclusive development in the future. Education and training must be improved and reoriented to emphasize the talents required for tomorrow's employment. With the outdated *learn-work-retire* model yielding to a new paradigm of lifelong learning, programs for worker upskilling and reskilling will become increasingly important.

Forward-thinking labor market policies should take precedence over trying to preserve existing employment, shifting the emphasis from defending current jobs to empowering employees to change jobs. Social safety nets will need to be strengthened to protect workers against the negative effects of technological change, and new models of work arrangements will need to be developed to ensure that workers share in the benefits of productivity growth. The key to winning the race with technology is not to compete against machines but to compete with machines.

3) The Growth of the Gig Economy

The gig economy is a term used to describe the trend of people working in short-term, contract-based jobs. This type of work is often done through online platforms, such as Uber or Airbnb. When the gig economy was first conceived in the United States, it was intended to be a stepping stone for individuals who were unemployed as a result of the Great Recession. However, the gig economy has become a permanent fixture in the American workforce, and it is estimated that nearly one-third of the workforce will be gig workers by 2030. This growth is being driven by several factors, including the rise of online platforms, the increasing use of temporary workers, and the declining cost of contracting work.

The gig economy has been criticized for its lack of job security and low wages. However, it has also been praised for its flexibility and ability to provide opportunities for those who are not able to find traditional employment. The gig economy is expected to continue to grow in the coming years, and it will likely have a significant impact on the American workforce. This could lead to more job insecurity and lower wages, as well as new opportunities for those who can take advantage of the gig economy.

Despite its reputation as being oriented toward low-skill and low-wage work, the gig- or talent-economy is far more diversified and professional than most people believe. A significant number of talent-economy employees have highly-specialized skills, such as coding, design, or marketing. The number of these types of workers has been growing rapidly, and they are often able to command high wages. The average hourly rate for gig economy workers is $28, compared to $21 for traditional workers. This difference is even more pronounced for highly-skilled workers, who can earn up to $60 per hour. As the coronavirus epidemic demonstrates, no organization or career is completely safe. At any moment, a firm may reorganize or cut staff.

With the globalization of business and recent advances in technology, businesses are increasingly reliant on running their operations with fewer full-time employees. Being a consultant or freelancer can be a high-growth opportunity for skilled workers—making them more valuable to employers. Traditional benefits for gig workers are on the rise. Several companies are offering health insurance, 401(k) plans, and other benefits to gig workers. These benefit packages are often more generous than what traditional workers receive. The trend toward benefits for gig workers is likely to continue, as companies compete for top talent in the increasingly tight labor market.

4) The Impact of Climate Change

There is broad consensus among scientists that human activities have caused atmospheric greenhouse gas levels to rise, and that this has contributed to a global average temperature increase. Overall negative economic consequences caused by climate change, including slow-onset and severe weather events, have been increasingly recognized by the United Nations Intergovernmental Panel. The economy is expected to be affected by climate change, particularly in specific industries such as housing, infrastructure, and agriculture.

Over one-third of the housing in the United States may be at high risk of climate-change-induced dangers, and billions of dollars' worth of property are at risk of destruction or unusability due to flooding hazards alone. A rise in sea level of just one meter is projected to put nearly 2 million American homes at risk of chronic flooding by the end of the century, and a 3.6 meter (*12 foot*) rise would put 11 million homes at risk. In New York City, a sea level rise of one meter would put more than 800,000 people and $200 billion in property at risk of flooding, and a three-meter rise would put 2.1 million people and $500 billion in property at risk.

The transportation infrastructure, which allows for the production and circulation of products and services, may be harmed by climate change. If the frequency and severity of extreme weather events continue to increase, then the risk will also increase. This means that the transportation system may not be able to handle as much extreme weather as it used to, which could cause problems. Storms, scorching heat, and other phenomena can wreak havoc on transportation systems, airports, and other infrastructure while adding to the production costs and disrupting consumption.

Agriculture may be severely impacted by climate change, leading to agricultural failures and increased food costs. The increased intensity of droughts and floods is expected to damage crops and disturb livestock. Drought, in particular, is a significant threat to agriculture. In the United States, for example, it is projected that climate change will reduce crop yields by 10% by 2050. This would have a significant impact on the food system, as well as on the economy.

Climate change will have a range of impacts on different sectors of the economy, some of which are difficult to predict. The overall impact of climate change is expected to be negative, with the potential to cause widespread economic damage. It is important to note that the effects of climate change will not be evenly distributed across regions or industries. Some areas and industries will be more impacted than others.

Despite the overall negative impact of climate change, there may be some sectors that benefit from the changes. For example, the increased intensity of hurricanes is expected to lead to more demand for construction and disaster-related services. In addition, as the world becomes warmer, some areas that are currently too cold for agriculture may become suitable for farming. A robust governmental response may create opportunities for new industries and jobs related to climate change mitigation or adaptation. For example, the United States government is investing in research and development of renewable energy sources, which could create new industries and jobs.

There are several ways to mitigate the effects of climate change, and it is important to take action to reduce the emissions of greenhouse gases. Mitigation strategies include: transitioning to renewable energy sources, improving energy efficiency, planting trees, and protecting natural ecosystems. In addition to mitigation, adaptation strategies are also important. These include: modifying infrastructure to be more resilient to extreme weather, developing drought-resistant crops, and relocating people out of harm's way.

5) The Rise of China

The United States has been the dominant economic power for centuries, but this is expected to change in the coming years. China is projected to overtake the United States as the world's largest economy, which could have far-reaching implications for the global economy and the balance of power. This could lead to more competition for jobs, as well as lower prices for goods and services. Like it or not, we are in a global economy and we must learn to compete in this new landscape.

For the United States to maintain its economic dominance, it will need to adapt to the rise of China. This will require a shift in thinking and policies. The United States must focus on creating an environment that is conducive to innovation and investment. Additionally, the United States must improve its education system and invest in research and development. Finally, the United States must strengthen its relationships with other countries, particularly those in Asia.

The rise of China is a challenge for the United States, but it is also an opportunity. As China's economy continues to grow, there will be more demand for goods and services. This offers a significant opportunity for businesses in the United States. If the United States can remain an attractive destination for investment and innovation, it will be well-positioned to benefit from the rise of China.

6) The Evolution of Money

Money is evolving as we move away from cash and toward digital currencies. This could lead to changes in the way we save, spend, and invest our money. In addition, it could also lead to new opportunities for those who can take advantage of the new financial system. Credit card and cell phone payments have disrupted the physical cash market already. As new cryptocurrencies become more popular, central banks will create their own more stable versions. Until such time, private companies will continue to lead the way in digital currencies.

What is digital currency? A digital or virtual currency is a type of money that is only available electronically. Bitcoin, Ripple, and Ethereum are all examples of digital currencies. These currencies are not backed by a central bank or government. Instead, they are backed by the network of computers that run the respective blockchain. While digital currencies hold some promise, they also come with risks. For example, digital currencies are not regulated by governments, which could make them more susceptible to fraud. Additionally, digital currencies are volatile, which means their value can fluctuate wildly. This makes them a risky investment.

Despite the risks, digital currencies are here to stay. They are becoming more popular and accepted as a form of payment. As such, it is important to understand how they work and how they could impact the economy. For example, digital currencies could lead to lower transaction costs and faster payment processing. Additionally, digital currencies could also make it easier for businesses to operate internationally. For the individual consumer, digital currencies offer an alternative to traditional banking.

7) The Green Revolution

The green revolution is a term used to describe the shift toward more environmentally-friendly practices. It is important to understand the implications of this shift so that you can be prepared for the changes that it will bring. This could include the use of renewable energy, the development of green technologies, and the adoption of sustainable practices. The green revolution is expected to lead to new jobs and industries, as well as opportunities for those who can take advantage of it. For example, those who are skilled in solar panel installation or wind turbine maintenance could find themselves in high demand. Additionally, those who can develop new green technologies could also find themselves in a position to profit.

Renewable energy is anticipated to play a major role in the green revolution. Solar, wind, and hydroelectric power are all renewable sources of energy. They are also environmentally friendly, as they do not produce greenhouse gases. The use of renewable energy is expected to increase in the coming years, as it becomes more affordable and reliable. This could lead to new jobs in the renewable energy sector. Additionally, it could also lead to lower electricity bills for consumers.

Green technologies include things like electric vehicles, green buildings, and energy-efficient appliances. These technologies are becoming more popular as we look for ways to reduce our impact on the environment. The adoption of green technologies is expected to lead to new jobs in the engineering and construction industries. Additionally, it could also lead to lower costs for consumers as we adopt more energy-efficient practices.

Sustainable practices are those that protect the environment while also meeting the needs of present and future generations. Sustainable practices include things like recycling, composting, and using renewable resources. The adoption of sustainable practices is expected to lead to new jobs in the waste management and environmental protection industries. Additionally, it could also lead to less pollution and a healthier environment for everyone.

Despite the benefits, the green revolution will also present some challenges. For example, the shift to renewable energy will require a significant investment in infrastructure. This could lead to higher taxes or utility rates. Additionally, the green revolution will also require changes in consumer behavior. For example, people will need to be willing to purchase electric vehicles and use less water. The green revolution will also require businesses to change the way they operate. For example, factories will need to become more efficient and waste will need to be reduced.

CHAPTER 7

This Land is Your Land

What is Community Wealth?

Woody Guthrie's folk anthem *This Land Is Your Land* has become an unofficial national anthem, standing the test of time with its powerful message of common ownership and a shared future, regardless of where we were born or who we are as individuals.

In an oligarchic society, wealth and resources are concentrated in the hands of a few. This often leaves the majority of people feeling left out and disenfranchised. But there is something we can do about it. We can build community wealth. Community wealth is created when everyone in a community has access to the resources they need to thrive. It is based on the idea that we are all connected, and that what benefits one member of the community benefits all members of the community. When we work together to create community wealth, we create a more just and equitable society for all.

Myths of Meritocracy: The Truth Behind Wealth Inequality

The classic American Dream was defined by upward mobility. The idea is that anyone, no matter their background or circumstances, can achieve success through hard work and determination. This dream was based on the premise that America is a meritocracy, where individuals are rewarded based on their ability and effort. The notion of a meritocracy—a social system in which power is distributed based on merit or achievement—is deeply ingrained in the American psyche. We like to believe that anyone, no matter their background, can achieve great things if they just work hard enough. Unfortunately, the data tell a different story. Wealth inequality is a very real problem in the United States, and it's only getting worse.

Supporters of meritocracy say that people like Andrew Carnegie, a Scottish immigrant who became very successful in America, are proof that the system works. They say that our current system of capitalism is the most effective way to allocate resources and spur economic growth. However, there are several problems with meritocracy in actual practice. It assumes that everyone has an equal chance to succeed. But in reality, people from wealthier backgrounds have a much better chance of getting ahead. They have access to better schools, neighborhoods, and networks. They can afford to take risks and make mistakes.

Assumptions about Meritocracy

Meritocracy assumes that hard work always leads to success. But this is not true for everyone. Many people work hard but don't get ahead. This system can often hide the biases that are built into the systems that determine who is talented and who is not. For example, standardized tests often favor people from wealthier backgrounds who can afford test prep and tutors. Meritocracy is a competitive system that does not take into account people's circumstances. For example, it does not adapt if someone has any disadvantages. It may also fail to evaluate the capacity to think differently or reliably assess talents in art, design, or social competencies where human judgment is so subjective. So while it may be the most efficient system for allocating resources, it's not necessarily the best system for all human beings.

Myth #1: Poor people are poor because they're lazy. The data shows that this simply isn't true. In fact, quite the opposite is true. Low-income Americans work more hours than ever before. A study by the National Employment Law Project found that 53% of low-wage workers are working more than 40 hours per week but are still living in poverty. The problem isn't that these workers aren't working hard enough; it's that they're not being paid enough for their labor.

Myth #2: The rich deserve their money because they worked hard for it. There's no denying that many wealthy people have worked hard to earn their money. But let's not forget that they also had a head start. The rich are more likely to come from wealthy families and to have access to resources that others do not. They're also more likely to have connections within their respective industries that can help them get ahead. Merit alone does not lead to success; opportunity does too.

Myth #3: Poverty is a result of bad personal choices. People living in poverty are often demonized for making *bad* personal choices, but the reality is that most of them are just trying to survive from day to day. They're making the best decisions they can with the limited resources they have available to them. Blaming poverty on personal choices ignores the systemic factors—like racism, sexism, and classism—that keep people trapped in a cycle of poverty.

Myth #4: Anyone can pull themselves up by their bootstraps. We like to believe that anyone can make something of themselves if they just try hard enough. But again, this simply isn't true. Wealth inequality is a very real problem in our society, and it makes it very difficult for people to move up the socioeconomic ladder. If you're born into a family with little money, it's going to be very difficult to become wealthy, no matter how hard you work.

Myth #5: Giving support to the poor just encourages laziness. There's a common belief that people living in poverty are lazy and that they're only looking for a handout. But this couldn't be further from the truth. Most people want to work and be self-sufficient. They just need a little help to get there. Assisting those in need not only helps to improve their lives, but also benefits society as a whole. When people can meet their basic needs, they're more likely to be productive citizens and less likely to rely on government assistance in the future.

So Why Does the Myth of Meritocracy Persist?

Part of the reason is that it's simply easier to believe that everyone has an equal chance at success than it is to face up to the harsh reality of inequality. After all, admitting that America is a country with high levels of inequality would require us to take action to address the problem. And that would be difficult and costly. It's also worth noting that the myth of meritocracy is perpetuated by those who benefit from it. The rich and powerful have a vested interest in maintaining the status quo because it benefits them at the expense of everyone else. As long as the myth of meritocracy persists, they can continue to amass more wealth and power while the rest of us fight for scraps.

Meritocracy Alternatives

The solution to these problems is not to get rid of meritocracy altogether. Rather, we need to make sure that everyone has an equal chance to succeed and that the systems that determine merit are fair. Regardless of how we fix the system, it's clear that meritocracy is not working the way it should. The first step is to dispel the myth that America is a meritocracy. It's simply not true. And once we accept that, we can start to take steps to address the problem.

Wealth inequality is a very real problem in the United States, and it's only getting worse. The myth of meritocracy—the belief that anyone can achieve success if they just work hard enough—persists despite evidence to the contrary. The truth is that many factors—including race, class, and gender—play a role in determining who succeeds and who doesn't. Ignoring these factors does a disservice to those who are struggling to make ends meet. It's time for us to start having honest conversations about wealth inequality in America and what we can do to close the gap between the haves and the have-nots.

What Is Community Wealth and Why Is It Important?

Practically everywhere you look, you'll see evidence of community wealth. It's the local coffee shop on the corner, the farmer's market down the street, and the family-owned restaurant that's been in business for generations.

Community wealth is all around us, but what does it really mean? And why is it important?

The term *community wealth* is frequently utilized but not fully understood. The resources available to a community to maintain itself are referred to as community wealth. Assets, such as land, infrastructure, businesses, cultural monuments, heritage sites, and people's relationships, are all examples of this. In a nutshell, community wealth is all of the resources, both tangible and intangible, that are owned by the members of a given community.

Community wealth is important because it allows a community to become self-sufficient and thrive. When a community has a strong base of community wealth, it means that the members of the community can work together to support each other and create a positive environment. It also allows communities to have greater control over their own destinies. When the members of a community own its wealth, they can make decisions about how that wealth should be used to benefit the community as a whole. This is in contrast to communities where the bulk of the wealth is owned by outsiders, who may not have the best interests of the community at heart.

A community with a strong foundation of community wealth is more economically stable and can better handle outside shocks. With global challenges like climate change and income inequality, our communities need to be as strong as possible. Robust levels of community wealth help to create more resilient communities. This is because when the members of a community own its wealth, they are less likely to be displaced when outside forces—such as economic downturns or natural disasters—threaten the stability of the community.

When businesses in the community are thriving, they can provide jobs for their residents. They can help to attract new businesses and residents to the area. When people see that a community has a lot to offer, they are more likely to want to be a part of it. This can help to increase tax revenues and also help to improve the local economy. Community wealth also has the potential to create greater equality within communities. This is because when the members of a community own its wealth, they can share in its benefits *(such as job creation or increased tax revenue)* more equitably.

A prosperous community can also benefit the physical environment by having a strong local economy. The presence of companies in the area is associated with better upkeep of buildings and the surrounding area. This improves the appearance of the entire neighborhood, allowing for even more businesses and residents to settle there. Reducing crime then helps to improve the quality of life for everyone in the area.

Not only do thriving local economies provide benefits to their residents, but they also benefit the larger society. An economically prosperous community is more likely to be politically stable. This is because people who have a stake in their community are more likely to want to protect it. They are also more likely to participate in the political process and work towards policies that benefit their community. When natural disasters or economic recessions occur, prosperous communities have the resources to bounce back without as much assistance from the government or outside organizations.

Community wealth is the foundation upon which strong, vibrant communities are built. By working together to create and maintain their own wealth, communities can have greater control over their destinies, become more resilient in the face of adversity, and create greater equality for all members of the community regardless of their background or circumstances. There are many ways to build community wealth, but it all starts with coming together and working towards common goals. We all have a role to play in building prosperous communities—let's get started!

Actionable Strategies for Building Community Wealth

One of the most important things happening today is the stark reality of growing inequality. This divide is evident not only in terms of income and assets, but also in terms of opportunity and access to quality education, healthcare, and housing. While this problem has been building for decades, it has come into even sharper relief in recent years as the wealthiest members of society have grown exponentially richer while the middle class continues to decline.

In an oligarchic society, the economic playing field is tilted decidedly in favor of those at the top, making it difficult for everyday Americans to get ahead. However, several strategies can be employed at the community level to start chipping away at this inequality and build real wealth for everyone, not just the privileged few.

Asset ownership is one of the most important determinants of wealth, yet the oligarchic structure of our economy makes it increasingly difficult for working-class and middle-class families to accumulate assets. A key way to begin rebuilding community wealth is therefore to ensure that everyone has a stake in owning property and other essential assets.

One way to do this is through community land trusts *(CLTs)*. CLTs are nonprofit organizations that purchase land and then lease it back to families, businesses, or other members of the community at an affordable rate. This model allows people to gain a foothold in the property market without being priced out by developers or speculators, while also ensuring that land remains accessible for future generations.

Another strategy for increasing asset ownership is worker-owned cooperatives. Cooperatives are businesses owned and controlled by their employees, who share in the profits *(or losses)* generated by the enterprise. Types of co-ops include worker cooperatives, housing cooperatives, food cooperatives, and credit unions. They are democratically run and operated for the benefit of their members, not for private profit. This model gives workers a direct stake in their company's success and allows them to share in the rewards generated by their labor. It also provides them with more control over their working conditions and job security, which helps to insulate them against economic downturns.

A third strategy for building community wealth is to invest in quality public goods and services. This includes everything from schools and parks to roads and public transit. When these services are adequately funded, they provide a benefit to everyone in the community, not just those who can afford to pay for private alternatives. Furthermore, public goods and services are often associated with increased property values, which can generate revenue that can be reinvested in the community.

These are just a few of the many strategies that can be used to start building community wealth in an oligarchic society. All of these things working together means that people have better wages, greater wealth equality, more stability in their work and family lives, more democratic communities, and better results for the environment and the planet's climate.

It is important to remember, however, that true wealth-building requires a fundamental shift in the way our economy is structured. Only by addressing the root causes of inequality will we be able to build an economy that works for everyone, not just the privileged few.

How Grassroots Activism Helps Build Community Wealth

A thriving local economy is good for everyone, but it's especially important for historically disadvantaged communities. That's because when wealth stays within the community, it helps to close the gap between rich and poor. It also gives people a sense of pride and ownership in their community. It's not just about money, it's about the resources that a community has to sustain itself.

Grassroots activism is essential for creating community wealth because it helps to build power from the ground up. When regular people work together to make change happen, they help create jobs, invest in their community, and make their voices heard. When people are empowered to create change, they are more likely to take pride in their community and invest in its future. They are also more likely to support local businesses and organizations, which in turn strengthens the local economy.

Grassroots Activism is More Than Just Raising Awareness

The concept of grassroots organizing believes that it is our responsibility to fix the problem instead of waiting for someone else to do so. There is power in numbers, and the more individuals we have working together, the more we can accomplish. We also have to be strategic in our approach. We can't just go out and start shouting about an issue; we need to have a plan and a goal in mind. We need to know who our target audience is and what we want to achieve. And we need to be willing to put in the hard work to make it happen. Grassroots organizing is about more than just raising awareness; it's about taking action and creating change. It's a powerful tool that can be used to effect positive change in our communities. And it starts with each of us taking responsibility for making our world a better place.

Grassroots Activism and Relationships

When people come together to fight for a common cause, they develop relationships and skills that can be used to effect change on other issues as well. Rather than viewing others as the enemy, they learn to see them as potential allies. They also learn how to work together effectively and how to navigate the political system. These skills and relationships are essential for creating long-term change. Grassroots activism is important not just for the issue at hand, but also for building power within the community. When people are empowered to create change, they take pride in their community and invest in its future. They also become better equipped to tackle other issues, creating a ripple effect of positive change.

Grassroots Activism and Politics

One of the most important roles of grassroots activists is holding elected officials accountable. We vote for these officials with the expectation that they will represent our best interests and fight for our communities. But too often, politicians are swayed by special interests or their own personal agendas. That's why it's so important to have regular citizens who are paying attention and holding them accountable. When constituents are engaged and involved, politicians are more likely to listen to their needs and fight for their interests. For example, if there's an issue with funding for public schools in your community, you can bet that your elected officials will be much more likely to do something about it if they're getting calls and emails from concerned citizens regularly. The same goes for issues like healthcare, housing, and environmental justice.

Starting a Grassroots Initiative

Grassroots organizing begins when someone spots an issue or problem. Then that person finds out who else is affected by the problem, as well as who may be interested in learning more about it, and brings them together in a small group. In this meeting, the group leader discusses her ideas and suggests a solution. The members then create a practical strategy. They consider who has the power to assist them and how they may reach out to them. They also look for anyone who might speak up on their behalf, particularly if they're able to reach out to someone of influence. The members of the group then attempt to contact individuals to get them involved. Communication is critical, using the media, especially social media, to connect with other like-minded individuals.

Identifying Issues for a Grassroots Movement

The first step in any grassroots organizing effort is to identify an issue or problem. This can be done by paying attention to what's going on in your community and the world around you. If you see something that isn't right or that could be improved, make a note of it. You can also talk to your friends and family, as well as other community members, to see if they're aware of any issues that need to be addressed. Once you've identified an issue, the next step is to research it and find out as much as you can. This will help you develop a better understanding of the issue and how it affects your community. It will also give you a chance to learn about potential solutions.

Reaching Out to Others in Your Community

After you've done your research, it's time to start reaching out to others who may be interested in getting involved. The best way to do this is to talk to people in your personal network, such as your friends and family. You can also reach out to community groups or organizations that may be working on similar issues. If you're not sure where to start, try attending a local government meeting or speaking with your elected officials. This can be a great way to learn about what's going on in your community and identify potential allies.

Developing a Grassroots Strategy

Once you've gathered a group of people who are interested in tackling the issue, it's time to start developing a strategy. The first step is to identify your goals. What do you hope to achieve by taking action? Once you've established your goals, you need to come up with a plan for how to achieve them. This will involve figuring out who has the power to help you achieve your goals and how you can reach out to them. You'll also need to consider what resources you have at your disposal and how you can best use them. Finally, you need to decide on a timeline for taking action.

Grassroots Action Planning

- Figure out what you're passionate about and find others who share your interest

- Connect with like-minded people through social media or in person

- Brainstorm ways to raise awareness about the issue and get people involved

- Create a plan of action and start taking steps to make your vision a reality

- Stay positive, organized, and motivated throughout the process

- Celebrate your successes along the way!

Grassroots activism is a powerful way to create community wealth and improve the quality of life for everyone in your community. By reaching out to others who share your interests, developing a strategy, and taking action, you can make a real difference in your community. To build community wealth, we need to level the playing field and create opportunities for everyone to participate. We need to ensure that everyone has a voice in decision-making and that the resources of our community are used for the benefit of all.

How to Identify the Key Players in Your Community

Getting things done in a community takes more than just effort, it takes organization. Regardless of where you live, your city or town has key players—the people who get things done. Knowing who the key players are in your area can make a big difference in terms of being effective. The key players are usually the people who are in positions of power, have a lot of connections, and are influential. If you can identify the key players in your community, you will be one step closer to getting things done.

There are a few different ways to identify the key players in your community. One way is to look for people who are involved in a lot of different organizations. These people are usually the ones who are well-connected and have a lot of influence. Talk to people in your community and see who is always involved in projects and getting things done. These are typically the people who are passionate about making a difference and they usually have a good network of contacts.

See who is always being mentioned in the local news. These are typically the people who are making positive changes in the community and they have a high profile. Check out local websites and social media groups. See who is always active and engaged in discussion. These people likely have a lot of influence in the community. Attend events or join clubs and organizations. Not only will you make some valuable connections, but you'll also learn more about what's going on in your town or city.

Consider the position, influence, and connections of the people you have identified. If you need something done at the city level, then you will want to look for someone who is in a position of power at the city level. If you need something done at the state level, then you will want to look for someone who is in a position of power at the state level. The same goes for the federal level. Keep in mind that it is often easier to get things done at the local level, so start there if possible. Look for people who advocate for the issues that you care about. These people are more likely to be receptive to your ideas and they will also have a better understanding of how to get things done.

Now that you have identified the key players in your community, it's time to start building relationships. The better your relationships are with the key players, the more likely you are to be successful in getting things done. Attend events, join clubs and organizations, and get involved in the community. Be sure to introduce yourself and let people know what you're passionate about. Build a rapport with the key players and always be respectful. You never know when you might need their help to get something done.

Ways to Get Involved in Community Wealth Building

Community wealth building is a term that refers to the creation and preservation of economic value within a specific geographical area. In other words, it's all about making sure that the money being earned in a community stays in that community to benefit its residents. There are many different ways to get involved in community wealth building. Here are several of them:

Invest in Local Businesses: One of the best ways to make sure that your community's wealth stays within its borders is to invest in local businesses. When you support businesses that are owned and operated by people who live in your community, you're helping to create jobs and spur economic growth. You can invest in local businesses by patronizing them, becoming a member of a cooperative, or investing money directly into their operations.

Support Local Farmers: When you buy locally grown food, you are supporting the farmers who live and work in your community. This helps to keep money within the community and also ensures that you are getting fresh, healthy food.

Develop Local Talent: This can be done by supporting educational initiatives, starting training programs, and providing opportunities for people to develop their skills and talents. When more people in your community can earn a good living, they'll be less likely to leave in search of opportunities elsewhere.

Build Social Capital: Social capital refers to the relationships between people within a community. Strong social ties make it more likely that people will help each other out and work together for the common good. You can build social capital by volunteering, joining community organizations, and getting to know your neighbors.

Advocate for PROGRESSIVE Policies: You can get involved in community wealth building by advocating for progressive policies at the local, state, and federal levels. Things like living wages, affordable housing, and quality public education are all key components of a healthy community. When people have access to these things, they're more likely to stay put and help contribute to the growth of their community.

Volunteer: By giving your time and energy, you can help make your community a better place for everyone. Volunteer opportunities abound, so there's sure to be something that fits your interests and skills. From tutoring kids to working on community gardens, there are many ways to get involved.

Give Back to the Community: This can be done in several different ways. For example, you could volunteer your time or donate money to a local organization that's working to improve the community. You could also invest your time and resources into mentoring someone who's interested in starting their own business. This is a great way to help someone achieve their dreams while also promoting entrepreneurship within the community.

Educate Yourself and Others About Community Wealth Building: This includes learning about the different ways you can get involved, as well as the impact that community wealth building can have on a community. It's also important to spread the word about community wealth building so that more people are aware of it and its benefits. The more people who are aware of it, the more likely it is that more people will get involved.

Community wealth building is an important way to ensure that economic value stays within a specific geographical area. There are many different ways to get involved, including investing in local businesses, developing local talent, building social capital, and advocating for progressive policies. What's most important is that you find a way that works best for you and your community.

What is the Role of Government in Community Wealth Building?

Government institutions provide the framework within which individuals, families, and businesses can interact with each other to create wealth. By creating and enforcing laws, regulating markets, and investing in public goods and services, governments ensure that communities have the resources they need to grow and prosper.

While some may argue that the government should stay out of the business of community wealth building, the reality is that without a strong government presence, communities would be far less wealthy. Consider, for example, the roads and highways that connect cities and towns. These are public infrastructure investments that would not be possible without government involvement. The same is true of schools, hospitals, and other vital services. By investing in these things, governments make it possible for communities to become wealthier and more prosperous.

There are several different ways that governments can promote community wealth building. One is by investing in public infrastructure, as mentioned above. This can include things like roads, bridges, and public transit. Here are additional ways that government can promote community wealth-building:

Providing Access to Capital: One of the biggest obstacles to starting a business is access to capital. By providing loans and other forms of financing, governments can help entrepreneurs get their businesses off the ground.

Establishing the Rule of Law: This means creating laws that protect citizens from violence, theft, and fraud. It also means enforcing those laws so that people feel safe and secure living in their communities. When people feel safe, they are more likely to take risks and start businesses. This helps to create jobs and spur economic growth.

Regulating Markets: This includes setting prices for things like utilities and transportation. It also means making sure that businesses are following consumer protection laws. By regulating markets, governments help to keep prices fair and prevent businesses from taking advantage of consumers.

Investing in Public Goods: Governments also invest in public goods such as education and infrastructure. These investments help to create jobs and spur economic growth. They also make it possible for businesses to thrive by providing them with a well-educated workforce and a good transportation system.

Ensuring Social Welfare: This includes providing safety nets for those who are unemployed or underemployed. It also means investing in health care and affordable housing. By doing this, governments help to reduce poverty and improve living conditions for all citizens.

Creating Jobs: These projects can include things like building roads or bridges, developing parks or recreation areas, or constructing new buildings or facilities. By putting people to work on these projects, governments help to stimulate the economy and create wealth within communities.

Partnering with Private Businesses: Governments often partner with private businesses to help finance and build community wealth-building projects, such as affordable housing developments or new schools. By working together, governments and businesses can leverage each other's resources to create projects that would not be possible. These partnerships help to attract investment, create jobs, and spur economic growth.

Establishing Municipal Enterprises: Municipal enterprises are businesses that are owned and operated by local governments. These businesses can provide a variety of services, such as child care, trash collection, or public transportation. They can also generate revenue for the government, which can be used to fund other community projects.

Developing Local Food Systems: This can include things like establishing farmers' markets, community gardens, or food hubs. It also means supporting local agriculture and promoting the consumption of locally-grown food. By developing local food systems, governments help to create jobs and spur economic growth. They also help to improve the health of citizens by providing them with access to fresh, healthy food.

Governments have several tools at their disposal that can help to promote community wealth building. By investing in public infrastructure, establishing the rule of law, regulating markets, and investing in public goods and services, governments can create an environment within which communities can thrive.

CHAPTER 8

Which Side Are You On?

Community Wealth Building Concepts

Which Side Are You On? by Florence Reece is a powerful song that speaks to the human struggle of deciding whether or not to join a cause. Composed in 1931, this union rallying cry captures the dilemma of staying safe on the sidelines while others march forward together, risking everything.

Community wealth building is a strategy for addressing inequality and creating more equitable and just societies. It involves building community-owned institutions and networks that generate economic activity and wealth within communities, rather than extraction of wealth from them. It's about taking back our economy from the 1% and reclaiming it for the 99%. It's about developing local economies where we can prosper and thrive because they're our economies. By focusing on inclusion, working collaboratively, cultivating local assets, and building new institutions, we can create economies we own and control and build community wealth for all of us. Community wealth building can take many forms, but all share a common goal: to increase the economic power and security of low- and moderate-income people and communities.

Community wealth building is a way to change the entire economic system, starting at the local level. This approach focuses on shared ownership and local decision-making about how to invest in and grow the local economy. It corrects the flaws of the economic theory known as trickle-down economics, which has been utilized by many nations throughout the world. It is a novel approach to economic development, poverty reduction, and equitable wealth creation and accumulation. In this approach, communities own and operate the major institutions and resources in the community. This helps people have more control over their community's capital and economic assets. These assets include cooperatives, community land trusts, municipal ownership, anchor strategies, public banks, and community-based financing. All of these things working together mean that people have better wages, greater wealth equality, more stability in their work and family lives, more democratic communities, and better results for the environment and the planet's climate.

Overview of Community Wealth Building Approaches

There are several ways to build community wealth. One is to create community development financial institutions *(CDFIs)*. CDFIs are private, nonprofit organizations that provide loans and investments to low- and moderate-income people and communities. They help people buy homes, start businesses, finance community projects, and more. Another way to build community wealth is through worker-owned cooperatives. Cooperatives are businesses owned and operated by the people who work there. They can be in any industry but are often in food service, health care, child care, and other service industries. Worker-owned cooperatives provide good jobs with benefits and a democratic workplace. They also keep money within the community, since the workers are also the owners.

Another way to build community wealth is through land trusts. Land trusts are nonprofit organizations that work to preserve land and make it affordable for people to live on. They do this by buying land and holding it in trust for the community. This keeps the land from being bought up by developers and turned into expensive housing or commercial property that only the wealthy can afford. Land trusts also develop affordable housing on the land they own, so that people of all income levels can have a place to live. There are many other ways to build community wealth. These are just a few examples. Community wealth building is a long-term process, and it takes time to see results. But it is a powerful way to address inequality and create more just and equitable societies.

Community Wealth Building Models

Cities all over the country are beginning to replicate and adapt a creative approach to economic development, environmental employment creation, and neighborhood revitalization. In some of the country's most economically-challenged cities, worker-owned and community-improvement businesses are starting to take root. These are businesses that are democratically controlled by their workers and/or the community, and they reinvest their profits back into the business or the local economy. There are many different models of worker-owned businesses, but all share a few common features:

- They are owned and controlled by the people who work there.

- They are businesses that provide goods or services to the community.

- They reinvest their profits back into the business or the local economy.

- They are democratic workplaces where everyone has a say in how the business is run.

- They are committed to improving the lives of their workers and the community.

The Cleveland Model

The Cleveland Model is a community wealth-building strategy that was developed in Cleveland, Ohio. It focuses on creating cooperative businesses and anchor institution investment in the city. The idea is to create jobs and keep money within the community. This helps to grow the economy and reduce inequality. The initial industries developed in this model were laundry services, renewable energy, urban agriculture, and media. Anchor institutions included universities, healthcare facilities, and cultural facilities; and education and training were organized and provided by a nonprofit organization.

The Mondragon Model

The Mondragon Model is a community wealth-building strategy that was developed in the Basque region of Spain. It focuses on creating worker-owned cooperatives. The Mondragon Cooperative Corporation is the largest worker-owned cooperative in the world. It includes over 100 cooperatives and employs over 80,000 people. The Mondragon Model has been successful in creating good jobs and reducing inequality. Knowledge, money, and consumer goods were the foundations for the early industries; later ones concentrated on industrial components and finance. The Catholic Church, coupled with a long-standing cooperative culture and a powerful labor movement, was an important anchor institution; and a local polytechnical school provided education and training.

The Portland Model

The Portland Model is a community wealth-building strategy that was developed in Portland, Oregon. It focuses on creating community-owned businesses. The idea is to keep money within the community and invest in local businesses. This helps to grow the economy and reduce inequality. The Portland Development Commission *(PDC)* worked with community partners in low-income areas, such as the nonprofit Native American Youth and Family Center, to launch a Neighborhood Prosperity Initiative in 2011. Six districts were created in areas with high concentrations of people of color and high poverty. Members of the community in each district developed a vision for improving their local commercial areas to promote economic development and neighborhood vitality. The city is attempting to develop in a way that is both inclusive and participatory.

The Stakeholder Model

The Stakeholder Model is a community wealth-building strategy that was developed by the Democracy Collaborative. It focuses on creating democratic workplaces. The idea is to give workers a say in how their workplace is run. This helps to create good jobs with benefits and a democratic workplace. The goal of this system is to replace the capitalist corporate system, which takes money away from local communities and gives it to a small elite, hurts the environment, embeds racism, and destroys our social fabric. In contrast, a democratic economy is a bottom-up approach to economic development based on greater democratic ownership, participation, and control at the local levels.

The Solidarity Economy

The solidarity economy is a worldwide movement committed to creating a just and sustainable economy that prioritizes people and the environment above profit and expansion. The solidarity economy emerged as a result of social movements in Latin America and the Global South. It provides genuine alternatives to capitalism through participatory democracy, cooperative and public ownership, and a culture of empathy and respect for the environment. The solidarity economy includes cooperative businesses, worker-owned cooperatives, land trusts, community development finance institutions, and more. The solidarity economy is a way to build community wealth and create more just and equitable societies.

Community Wealth Building Concepts

The following are some key concepts and strategies associated with community wealth building in the solidarity economy. It should be understood that the individual components work together as a complete system, rather than as isolated parts. For example, a cooperative business cannot be successful without a supportive legal and regulatory framework. Employers, purchasers, land and property owners, and financial investors all have a role to play in creating and sustaining the solidarity economy. The rules and principles of the solidarity economy are vastly different than those of the capitalist economy. In the solidarity economy, for example, businesses are not concerned with profit maximization; instead, they aim to fulfill the needs of the community. The shareholders of a cooperative are the workers, not outside investors. Increased local consumption, rather than taking money and employment away from the region's economy, generates additional employment. This creates a *multiplier effect* which will lead to even more jobs due to increased demand for local goods and services. Employees and communities benefit in new and innovative ways when this money is invested in ways that are beneficial to widely-held, socially-aware businesses, workers, and communities.

Anchor Institutions

Anchor institutions are large organizations that are rooted in a community. They can be hospitals, universities, foundations, or any other type of organization. Anchor institutions have the power to make changes in a community. They can use their power and influence to create jobs, support small businesses, and invest in the community. They help to stabilize communities and make them more resilient because they're not as likely to leave as other businesses. Anchor institutions can use their power and influence to support community wealth-building. For example, they can invest in worker-owned cooperatives or land trusts. They can also support small businesses and entrepreneurs. They can provide loans and investments to help them get started and grow. They can also help to create jobs by hiring workers from the community.

Community Development Corporations (CDCs)

Community development corporations are nonprofit organizations that work to revitalize neighborhoods and create economic opportunities. They do this by developing affordable housing, supporting small businesses, providing job training, enabling commercial development, and delivering healthcare and other social programs. CDCs are responsible for developing community wealth, since they anchor funds in local communities, allow for grass-roots involvement in decision-making, and give residents the ability to acquire more political influence. Many CDCs grew out of the Civil Rights movement to fight against redlining and divestment issues in cities. Redlining is a prohibited discriminatory act in which a mortgage lender or an insurance provider refuses loans or services to specific sections of a community, frequently because of the racial makeup of the applicant's neighborhood.

Community Development Financial Institutions (CDFIs)

Community Development Financial Institutions (*CDFIs*) are private financial institutions that work to increase economic opportunities in underserved communities. They do this by providing capital to small businesses, nonprofits, and community development projects. CDFIs are often community-based organizations with a mission to serve low-income people and communities of color. They are an important source of financing for community wealth-building projects. They specialize in lending to individuals, businesses, and organizations in under-resourced communities. They offer clients financial education, business coaching, and low-interest rate loans to increase their economic potential and build wealth. CDFI loans promote local development and small business growth, as well as home ownership, provide living-wage employment, help to build schools, grocery stores, and health care centers, support climate change initiatives, and much more.

Community Land Trusts (CLTs)

Community Land Trusts (*CLTs*) are nonprofits that work to increase community control of land and housing. They do this by acquiring land and developing it for affordable housing, small businesses, community gardens, or other community needs. CLTs keep the land in trust so that it can be used for the good of the community rather than for private profit. This protects the affordability of the housing and ensures that the land is used for the benefit of future generations. CLTs are an important tool for building community wealth because they allow communities to pool their resources and have a say in how their neighborhoods are developed.

Cooperatives (Co-ops)

Cooperatives (*Co-ops*) are businesses that are owned and controlled by the people who use their services. Types of co-ops include worker cooperatives, housing cooperatives, food cooperatives, and credit unions. They are democratically run and operated for the benefit of their members, not for private profit. Co-ops can be businesses of any size, from small worker-owned businesses to large consumer cooperatives. Co-ops provide their members with benefits such as economic democracy, social cohesion, and economic sustainability. Co-ops are an important part of the solidarity economy because they allow people to pool their resources and have more control over their work lives.

Cooperatives have a long history in the United States, dating back to the 18th century. Today, there are over 30,000 cooperatives in the country, with over 120 million members. The cooperative movement has been particularly successful in rural areas, where they have helped to create jobs and provide essential services. Despite their successes, cooperatives face significant challenges. They are often located in economically disadvantaged areas, which can make it difficult to access capital. They also tend to be small businesses, which can make them vulnerable to competition from larger companies. In addition, cooperatives often have difficulty scaling up their operations and expanding into new markets.

Cross-Sector Collaboration

Cross-Sector Collaboration is a process in which organizations from different sectors work together to solve a problem or achieve a common goal. This can be done through formal partnerships, joint ventures, or simply by sharing resources and expertise. Cross-sector collaboration is important for community wealth building because it allows different organizations to pool their resources and create more comprehensive solutions to problems. Examples of cross-sector collaboration include public-private partnerships, social impact bonds, and community benefit agreements.

Economic Development

Economic Development is a process by which a community or region improves the economic well-being of its residents. This can be done through initiatives such as job creation, business development, and workforce training. Economic development is an important part of community wealth building because it increases the overall prosperity of a community and allows residents to have more economic opportunities.

Employee Stock Ownership Plans (ESOPs)

Employee Stock Ownership Plans (*ESOPs*) are a type of retirement plan that allows employees to own shares of their company. ESOPs are a way for employees to build wealth and have a say in the future of their company. They can also help to keep companies locally owned and increase employee productivity. ESOPs are an important tool for community wealth building because they allow workers to share in the benefits of company growth.

Enterprise Zones

Enterprise Zones are areas that have been designated by the government as having special economic development benefits. These benefits can include tax breaks, infrastructure improvements, and regulatory exemptions. Enterprise Zones are an important part of community wealth building because they attract investment and encourage business development in under-resourced communities.

Equitable Development

Equitable Development is a process by which all members of a community share in the benefits of economic growth. This includes ensuring that low-income residents have access to quality jobs, housing, and schools. Equitable development is an important part of community wealth building because it ensures that everyone has a chance to benefit from economic prosperity.

Fair Trade

Fair Trade is a system of trade that promotes equitable working conditions and environmental sustainability. Fair-trade certified products must meet certain standards, such as being produced without child labor or forced labor. Fair trade is an important part of the solidarity economy because it supports workers' rights and sustainable production. Fair trade products include coffee, chocolate, sugar, and bananas.

Family-Owned Businesses

Family-Owned Businesses are businesses that are owned and operated by members of the same family. Family-owned businesses are an important part of the solidarity economy because they are often locally owned and operated. They can also provide good jobs and economic stability for families. Many Americans who are descendants of families without a long history of capital access may find it difficult to accumulate wealth for future generations. However, the road to financial success for your family, like many of America's most renowned families, must begin somewhere, and it might start with you. Financial success for your family may mean that your children, grandchildren, and their children at the very least get a decent chance at financial success. Something as simple as being able to graduate debt-free can put your child on a path to a secure and stable future.

Green Economy

The green economy is an economy that is based on environmental sustainability. Green jobs are jobs that help to protect the environment, such as jobs in renewable energy, green building, and environmental conservation. The green economy is a vital component of the solidarity economy since it creates employment that is beneficial to the environment while also protecting our natural resources. Green-collar jobs are jobs that help the environment and also pay well. They are a good way to move low-income workers into better-paying jobs. A green-collar job might be working in a solar panel factory, or helping to install solar panels on people's homes. Or, it could be working in a recycling plant, or helping to clean up a polluted river. Green collar jobs are important because they help to protect the environment, and they also provide good jobs for people who want to work in an industry that is beneficial to society.

Impact Investing

Impact Investing is a type of investing that seeks to generate positive social and environmental impact as well as financial return. Impact investments can be made in both for-profit and non-profit organizations. Impact investing is an important part of the solidarity economy because it allows investors to support businesses and organizations that are working to make a positive difference in the world. Socially Responsible Investments *(SRIs)* are investment strategies that individuals employ to generate financial returns while promoting social good. SRIs take into account environmental, social, and governance *(ESG)* factors when making investment decisions. Many impact investors use SRI strategies to screen companies and organizations in which they might invest. Program-related investments *(PRIs)* are used by foundations and anchor institutions to provide long-term, low-interest loans to promote community wealth building and other mission-related foundation goals.

Individual Wealth Building

Individual wealth-building is a community wealth-building approach that focuses on helping individuals save money, invest in assets, and become financially secure. The Individual Development Account *(IDA)* is one tool that can be used for individual wealth building. IDAs are savings accounts that match the money saved by the account holder. For every dollar saved, the account holder receives a match from the IDA provider. The match can be in the form of cash, or it can be in the form of services, such as training or technical assistance. The IDA program is a way to help low-income individuals save money and build wealth. Savers agree to take classes about finance and then use their savings for a good purpose, like education, small business finance, or buying a house.

Individual Wealth Preservation

Individual Wealth Preservation is the process of protecting your wealth from things like inflation, taxes, and unexpected events. Financial literacy, foreclosure prevention, programs to *bank the unbanked*, activism and policy efforts to restrict predatory lending, and tax refund assistance are just a few of the ways to preserve individual wealth. Asset protection is a type of individual wealth preservation that involves creating legal structures, such as trusts, to protect your assets from creditors and lawsuits. Insurance is another type of individual wealth preservation that can protect you from financial losses due to accidents, death, or illness.

Local Assets

Local assets are the resources that a community has. They can be natural resources, like land or water. They can also be human resources, like the skills and knowledge of the people who live there. Local assets can be used to create wealth and jobs in the community. For example, a community might have a lot of unused land. A land trust could buy this land and develop it into affordable housing or a community garden. This would create jobs and provide a service to the community. The key to creating wealth in any community is to first assess what local assets are available, and then put them to use in a way that will benefit the community as a whole. Community wealth building is a long-term process, but it is a powerful way to create more just and equitable societies.

Local Food Systems

A local food system is a collaborative network of farmers and food businesses that produce, process, distribute, and consume food that is grown or produced locally. Local food systems create economic opportunities for small farmers, food businesses, and consumers. They also promote environmental stewardship and public health. Local food systems are an important part of the community wealth-building movement. They offer a way to create jobs and wealth in communities while also promoting local economic development.

Municipal Enterprise

Municipal enterprises are businesses owned by local governments. They can be used to provide services or generate revenue for the city or county. Municipal enterprises are a type of public-private partnership. They offer the benefits of private enterprise, such as flexibility and innovation, while also providing the stability and accountability of government ownership. Municipal enterprises can be used to create jobs and wealth in the community. For example, a city might start a municipal enterprise to provide high-speed internet service to businesses and residences. This would create jobs for installation and maintenance technicians, and it would generate revenue for the city.

New State & Local Policies

For community wealth building to be successful, states and localities must create policies that support it. For example, states can create policies that encourage the development of local food systems. Localities can create policies that allow for the creation of municipal enterprises. Other policy changes that are needed to support community wealth-building include:

- Increasing the minimum wage

- Expanding access to affordable housing

- Investing in public infrastructure

- Improving access to capital for small businesses

- Reforming the tax code to promote investment in communities

These are just a few examples of the types of policy changes that are needed to support community wealth building. The important thing is that states and localities work together to create a supportive policy environment for community wealth building.

Reclaiming Common Resources

Reclaiming the commons is the process of taking back control of common resources, such as land, water, and air, from private interests. The commons are resources that we all share and have a right to use. They are essential to our survival and well-being. Reclaiming the commons is a way to protect these resources for future generations. It is also a way to create jobs and wealth in the present. For example, a community might come together to buy a parcel of land that is threatened by development. This land could then be used for sustainable agriculture, recreation, or conservation. The key to reclaiming the commons is to build community power. This can be done through organizing, education, and political action.

Social Capital

Social capital is the relationships and networks that people have with each other. It's what allows us to trust and cooperate. Social capital is important for community wealth building because it helps people come together to work on common goals. It also helps build social cohesion and trust, which are important for a community to function well. It reverses the *divide-and-conquer* strategy that is used by those in power to keep us from working together. Social capital can be built through organizing, education, and political action.

Social Enterprise

Social enterprises have become more common over the past three decades because of government funding cuts to social programs. Goodwill Industries, the Girl Scouts, and the YMCA are all prominent examples of social enterprises. Goodwill began by employing poor, city residents to repair and sell donated goods, and then used the revenues generated to fund its community and job training programs. Social enterprises are businesses that have a social or environmental mission. They are often started by nonprofits, but they can also be started by for-profit businesses. Social enterprises can be used to create jobs and wealth in the community. For example, a social enterprise might start a business to provide job training and employment services to people with criminal records. This would create jobs for the staff of the enterprise, and it would also provide valuable services to the community.

Solidarity Economy

The Solidarity Economy is an economy that is based on principles of solidarity, cooperation, and social justice. The solidarity economy includes a wide range of economic activity, from community-owned businesses to cooperative organizations to fair trade. The solidarity economy is an important part of the community wealth-building movement because it offers an alternative to the traditional capitalist economy. The solidarity economy is based on the idea that our economic system should be based on cooperation, not competition. It should be based on the needs of people and the planet, not on profits.

State and Local Investments

State and local investments are an important source of funding for community wealth-building initiatives. State and local governments can invest in a wide range of community development projects, such as affordable housing, green infrastructure, and small business development. State and local governments can also create programs to support community wealth building.

Transit-Oriented Development

Transit-oriented development (*TOD*) is a type of development that is designed around public transportation. TOD projects typically include a mix of residential, commercial, and retail space. TOD can be used to create jobs and wealth in the community. It can also help reduce traffic congestion and pollution, and it can make it easier for people to get around without a car. TOD is made possible by regional or local governments that encourage it through land use planning, zoning laws, and changes to building codes, among other things.

Urban Agriculture

Urban agriculture is the practice of growing food in an urban environment. Urban agriculture can be used to create jobs and wealth in the community. It can also help to improve the food security of the community, and it can provide fresh, healthy food to residents. Urban farming might take the form of backyard, rooftop, and balcony gardening, as well as community gardening in vacant lots and parks, roadside urban fringe agriculture, livestock grazing in open space, and intensive indoor hydroponic or aquaculture farms. Urban agriculture enables people to have direct access to food, reconnects communities to the act of growing it, and engages the community on several levels.

University & Community Partnerships

University and community partnerships are an important part of the community wealth-building movement. Partnerships between universities and communities can help to create jobs and wealth in the community. They can also help to improve the quality of life for residents, and they can provide opportunities for students to get involved in the community. Examples of university and community partnerships include university-sponsored business incubators and accelerators, community service-learning programs, and research collaborations.

Worker Cooperatives

Worker cooperatives are businesses that are owned and controlled by the workers. Worker cooperatives can be used to create jobs and wealth in the community. They can also help to improve the quality of life for workers, and they can provide opportunities for employees to become owners. Many worker cooperatives that exist today were inspired by the Mondragon Cooperatives in Spain. These cooperatives helped the Basques escape poverty and build a strong economy. There is growing interest in worker cooperatives as a way to create jobs and build wealth. Community organizations, cities, and small business advocates see potential in worker cooperatives to create a more inclusive economy.

CHAPTER 9

Imagine

Collective Action in a Divided World

John Lennon's song *Imagine* speaks of a world without the divisions of religion, possessions, and culture that lead to greed and war. Lennon uses repetition of the word *imagine* to emphasize his message of hope for a better world through our collective action.

Across the United States, there are inspiring examples of community wealth-building projects that have successfully mobilized residents to achieve common goals. From creating cooperatives to establishing community land trusts, these initiatives have strengthened communities while building a foundation for sustainable economic growth. This effort has been driven in part by the recognition that our economy is not working for everyone. While a select few have benefited immensely from economic growth, the majority of Americans have been left behind. Inequality has reached record levels, and the middle class is shrinking. This reality has led to a growing sense of frustration and anger, which has manifested in political populism and social unrest.

In response to this, several organizations and individuals have begun experimenting with new approaches to community development. These initiatives seek to create wealth and opportunity from the bottom up, rather than relying on trickle-down economic growth. They are based on the belief that when people come together and work toward common goals, they can create something much greater than what any one individual could achieve alone. Despite their successes, however, many such projects face significant challenges in the current political and economic climate. To realize their full potential, we must support and learn from these innovative initiatives.

The Power of Collective Action in a Divided World

In a world of increasing division, collective action is more important than ever. Building strong and vibrant communities requires us to come together and confront the underlying causes of inequality. Only by doing so can we create a system of community wealth and social change that will benefit everyone, regardless of their background or identity. This means looking beyond individual success to focus on our collective responsibility for the well-being of all.

The Evergreen Cooperatives in Cleveland, Ohio

The Evergreen Cooperatives in Cleveland, Ohio are a group of worker-owned businesses that provide green products and services to the local community. These businesses include a laundry, a solar panel installation company, an urban farm, and a commercial printing business. The Evergreen Cooperatives were founded in 2009 in response to the loss of manufacturing jobs in the city. By providing good jobs and training opportunities for residents, the Evergreen Cooperatives are working to revitalize Cleveland's economy from the bottom up.

The cooperative model has several advantages over traditional businesses. For one, it allows workers to share in the profits of the business, rather than simply being paid wages. This gives employees a greater sense of ownership and responsibility, and encourages them to work harder and be more productive. In addition, cooperative businesses are typically more responsive to the needs of their community than traditional businesses, as they are democratically controlled by the people who live and work there.

The Evergreen Cooperatives have been successful in creating good jobs and revitalizing Cleveland's economy. However, they have faced several challenges along the way. One challenge is the lack of access to capital. Because they are new and relatively small businesses, the Evergreen Cooperatives have had difficulty securing loans from traditional banks. They have also been hurt by the decline of the city's population, as this has led to a decrease in demand for their products and services. Despite these challenges, the Evergreen Cooperatives have continued to grow and expand their impact.

Community Land Trust in Denver, Colorado

The Community Land Trust is a nonprofit organization that works to ensure that the community maintains control of the land on which it sits. The Land Trust accomplishes this by holding the title to the land in trust for the community, rather than allowing individuals or developers to own it. This ensures that the land remains affordable and accessible to everyone in the community. The Land Trust model has several advantages over traditional development. For one, it allows communities to control the development of their neighborhoods. This ensures that new development meets the needs of the community, rather than benefiting outside developers or investors. In addition, the Land Trust model keeps the land affordable for everyone in the community.

The Land Trust was founded in 2002 in response to the rapid gentrification of the neighborhood. As property values began to rise, many longtime residents were being priced out of their homes. The Land Trust was created to prevent this from happening and to ensure that the community remained diverse. The Land Trust has been successful in preserving the affordability and diversity of the neighborhood. However, it has faced several challenges along the way. One challenge is that the Land Trust's properties are not exempt from property taxes, which puts a financial burden on the organization. In addition, the Land Trust has had difficulty acquiring new properties, as many of the landowners in the neighborhood are not willing to sell their land to the organization. Despite these challenges, the Community Land Trust has continued to grow and expand its impact.

Dudley Street Neighborhood Initiative in Boston, Massachusetts

Dudley Street Neighborhood Initiative in Boston, Massachusetts is a community-based organization that works to revitalize the Dudley Street neighborhood. The organization was founded in 1984 by Dudley residents seeking to reclaim a neighborhood that had been ravaged by disinvestment, disrepair, arson fires, and dumping that had plagued the area for decades. To secure development without displacement, DSNI gained eminent domain authority, purchased vacant land, and protected affordability. Through a combination of community organizing, youth development, and economic development, the Dudley Street Neighborhood Initiative has been successful in turning the neighborhood around. When many had given up, DSNI organized neighbors to create a comprehensive plan and a shared vision for a new, vibrant urban village. The organization has helped to create affordable housing, develop new businesses, and improve the quality of life for residents. However, it has faced several challenges along the way. One challenge is that the organization has been unable to secure enough funding to maintain all of its programs and services. In addition, the Dudley Street neighborhood is still considered to be a high-crime area, which has made it difficult to attract new residents and businesses. Despite these challenges, the Dudley Street Neighborhood Initiative has continued to grow and expand its impact.

The Community Development Corporation of Long Island in Hempstead, New York

The Community Development Corporation of Long Island (*CDCLI*) in Hempstead, New York is a nonprofit organization that works to revitalize struggling communities on Long Island. The organization was founded in 1971 in response to the decline of many Long Island communities. Through a combination of community organizing, economic development, and housing development, the CDC of Long Island has been successful in turning around several communities. The organization has helped to create affordable housing, develop new businesses, and improve the quality of life for residents. CDCLI invests in the housing and economic aspirations of individuals and families by providing solutions that foster and maintain vibrant, equitable, and sustainable communities. It is a chartered member of NeighborWorks®, a nationwide network of more than 240 trained and certified community development organizations at work in nearly 4,000 communities across America. Working in partnership with others, NeighborWorks organizations are leaders in revitalizing communities.

New Era Community Connection

New Era Community Connection (*NECC*) is a family movement of New Era Nation that was designed exclusively to connect and develop urban communities worldwide through an original *mudroots* concept, direct outreach, and hands-on community programming to assist in creating an environment of self-sufficiency throughout often forgotten communities. New Era strives to instill self-reliance and community stewardship in the next generation of Black kids so that they may see how to create the life we want to live as a people. New Era is operating 15 programs based on five levels of accountability:

- **Self Accountability:** It's essential to look at ourselves and make sure we're prepared. If you can't face yourself in the mirror and hold yourself accountable, nothing or no one will be held accountable.

- **Household Accountability:** We need to make sure that the people around us are doing their best. If we try to raise our vibrations but the people around us don't try to do the same, it won't work.

- **Community Accountability:** We must continue to educate ourselves and others so that we can become better-informed participants in our own lives and communities, as well as hold those who run them accountable.

- **Economic Accountability:** There are a lot of things we can do to help our communities. We can make sure that we are spending money with black businesses, opening black businesses, and making sure that we understand credit and finances. We can also put money back into our own communities.

- **Political Accountability:** People need to understand that politics is involved in everything. It's important to be educated on the political process so that we can elect people who are qualified and represent our communities well. We need to know who to hold accountable and how to hold them accountable to make positive changes in our world.

New Economy Coalition

New Economy Coalition (*NEC*) is a network of organizations and individuals working to build an economy that works for all. The New Economy Coalition is made up of over 200 member organizations from across the United States that believe in an economy rooted in justice, democracy, and ecological sustainability. NEC's members come from a variety of organizations, including mission-driven firms, grassroots community groups, and sectoral associations. Many organizations join NEC to be a part of a cross-sectoral and national network, even though they specialize in a certain approach or are based in a particular geographic location. NEC was founded in 2012 on the heels of the Great Recession, in response to growing national interest in solidarity economy practices, values, and strategies for systemic change. In 2016, they began to transition from a largely white, upper-class organization to one with a majority of people of color and considerably more geographically and socioeconomically diversified employees.

The Federation of Southern Cooperatives/Land Assistance Fund in Alabama

The Federation of Southern Cooperatives/Land Assistance Fund in Alabama is a non-profit cooperative association of black farmers, landowners, and cooperatives. The majority of their farmers, landowners, cooperatives, and credit unions are in Georgia, Mississippi, Alabama, Florida, and Louisiana. The Federation was founded by community organizations and leaders who had been shaped and formed in the Civil Rights Movement of the 1960s. These people knew that for their community development project to be successful, they needed to show progress through alternative means and also advocate for change in public policies that would help support their project. Over the years, the Federation has worked to advocate for public policies that would assist Black farmers and develop persistently impoverished rural areas at the local, state, and federal levels. Even though the number of Black farmers and landowners in the South has dwindled from over 100,000 to less than 20,000 today, the Federation continues to collaborate with scores of these landholders.

Cooperation Jackson in Jackson, Mississippi

Cooperation Jackson is a network of worker-owned cooperatives and support organizations in Jackson, Mississippi that is committed to building a solidarity economy. They are inspired by the Mondragon Cooperatives in the Basque region of Spain and the worker-cooperative movement in the United States. Cooperation Jackson was founded in 2013 by Kali Akuno, who served as the Director of Special Projects and External Funding in the mayorship of Chokwe Lumumba. After Lumumba's passing, Akuno resigned from his post to start Cooperation Jackson as a way to continue Lumumba's vision for economic development in Jackson. Cooperation Jackson is working to build an ecosystem of worker-owned cooperatives that are rooted in the principles of solidarity, democracy, and sustainability. They are also working to create a cooperative incubator and business association to support the growth of worker-owned cooperatives in Jackson.

New Communities Program in Albany and Atlanta, Georgia

New Communities Program (*NCP*) is a long-term program that was created to help African American farmers keep their land and build wealth in the rural south. In 1968, after years of working with the Student Nonviolent Coordinating Committee (*SNCC*), civil rights leader Robert F. Kennedy visited the Albany Freedom Farm Cooperative in Albany, Georgia. This visit was a turning point for the NCP, which began as a response to the plight of the Freedom Farmers. The program was designed to help the Freedom Farmers and other African American farmers in the rural south to keep their land and build wealth. Over the years, the NCP has helped to develop more than 20 community-owned businesses and over 2,000 housing units. The NCP is currently headquartered in Atlanta, Georgia and has a staff of over 60 people.

The South Bronx Community Congress in New York City

The South Bronx Community Congress is a membership organization of low- and moderate-income residents of the South Bronx. The Congress was founded in 1974 as a response to the economic crisis that was ravaging the South Bronx. Since then, the Congress has been working to build community power and improve the quality of life for residents of the South Bronx. The

Congress is involved in many different aspects of community life, including housing, education, economic development, and health.

The North Carolina Mutual Aid Society in Durham, North Carolina

The North Carolina Mutual Aid Society is a membership organization that was founded in 1898 to provide financial assistance to African Americans in the state of North Carolina. The Society is still in operation today and has helped thousands of families with financial assistance, scholarships, and loans. The Society is also involved in community development and has helped to finance the construction of several community facilities, including the North Carolina Mutual Life Insurance Company Building and the Durham County Human Services Building.

Foundation Communities

Foundation Communities was created in 1990 to help low-income families and individuals. It has become a national leader in the asset-building movement. The organization runs over 20 low-income housing communities with over 2,800 low-income residents in Austin and North Texas. Their housing model is designed to help people break the cycle of poverty. The model includes on-site service centers which offer programs like financial literacy and education. The program also offers a matched savings program. For every $1 that someone saves, the program will match it with $2. The money can be used to purchase a home, college tuition, or small business expansion.

Recology

Recology is a 100-percent employee-owned company dedicated to building resource ecosystems that protect the environment and sustain communities. The goal of the Recology business is to promote resource recovery as a replacement for conventional waste management. They work to stop resources from going to waste by developing sustainable practices that can be used all around the world. Recology hires directly from the communities it serves, aims to purchase local goods and services when possible, and supports community development programs. In 1986, the company switched to an Employee Stock Ownership Plan (*ESOP*), so that Recology would be 100% employee-owned. Recology employees are more committed to the company, its goals, and customer satisfaction in the communities where they operate as a result of its being 100-percent employee-owned. Recology makes sure that their workers have a good retirement. They offer a supplemental retirement plan alongside their 401(*K*) or pension, as well as a comprehensive benefits package.

Equity Trust

Equity Trust is a small, national nonprofit organization helping communities to gain ownership interests in land and other local resources. They strive to bring about economic changes that will satisfy both individuals and the collective community, while being environmentally sustainable and considerate of future generations. Their Farms for Farmers initiative encourages different types of farmland ownership that would help farmers needing affordable land and areas wishing to have a local, sustainable food source while also conserving the environment. Their Equity Trust Fund is a loan fund that allows socially aware lenders and donors to contribute to projects that are developing new property ownership, usage, and stewardship methods. Their Property and Values program encourages people to learn about, understand, and put into action economically just ways of owning property that prioritize social justice, fairness, and sustainability.

Pike Place Market

Pike Place Market is a historic public market that has been operating since 1907, housing hundreds of farmers, crafters, small businesses, and residents. This municipal enterprise was created to preserve, rehabilitate, and operate the Market as a public trust on behalf of the people of Seattle. Municipal enterprises play a critical role in building community wealth by creating good jobs, generating revenue for vital public services, and anchoring local economies. The Pike Place Market is a great example of how a municipal enterprise can be used to build community wealth. The Market generates millions of dollars in revenue annually, which helps to fund vital public services such as police and fire protection, and parks and recreation. The Market also anchors the local economy by attracting visitors and tourists, which supports other businesses in the area. The Market is currently operated and managed by the Pike Place Market Preservation & Development Authority *(PDA)*, a not-for-profit, public corporation established in 1973 by the City of Seattle.

Community Reinvestment Fund

Established in 1988, Community Reinvestment Fund, USA *(CRF)* is a nationwide non-profit organization committed to enhancing lives and empowering communities through innovative financial solutions. As a leading Community Development Financial Institution *(CDFI)*, CRF strives to increase the financial flow to communities that have experienced consistent underinvestment by developing products and services for mission-driven organizations. CRF and its partners are using community development finance to build more resilient local economies, promote employment growth, and help people move up the economic ladder. That translates into more business start-ups, more funding for business expansions, more resources for hiring and retaining talent, and greater economic empowerment for everyone living and working in under-invested communities.

The Park Slope Food Coop

The Park Slope Food Coop is a member-owned and operated cooperative food store in Brooklyn, New York. It is an alternative to commercial profit-oriented business models, and is based on the principles of cooperation, democracy, equality, and social justice. The Coop was founded in 1973 with just a few dozen members, and has since grown to over 16,000 members. It is open to the public, and anyone can become a member by working a shift in the store. One of the Coop's goals is to provide food to the member-owners that is both low-priced and high-quality. Members do about 75% of the work, thereby keeping payroll expenses low, which is the main reason that the members of this Coop pay low prices. When members are doing 75% of the work in a co-op, they feel more like owners than investors. This sense of ownership is something that money cannot buy. The multifaceted role of member as worker, owner, and shopper fosters a sense of belonging and community that is rare in the corporate food world.

The ICA Group

The ICA Group is a leading expert on worker ownership and the oldest national organization dedicated to the development of worker cooperatives. Since 1977, ICA has launched dozens of worker-owned cooperatives and social enterprises, helped dozens of companies convert to worker ownership, and created and preserved over 10,000 jobs. ICA has fostered worker ownership networks in the home-care and child-care industries, and has developed two programs that concentrate on maintaining businesses whose owners are seeking to retire. They have developed technical assistance tools and procedures, partnered with key community and industry groups, and identified successful worker-owned businesses who can act as champions and advocates for worker ownership.

These are just a few examples of how people are coming together to create wealth and opportunity in their communities. When people unite, they have the power to create real change. Collectively, we can build a more just and equitable world.

CHAPTER 10

Mercy Mercy Me

Opportunities in the Solidarity Economy

Mercy Mercy Me by Marvin Gaye is a powerful plea for environmental awareness that was released long before the environmental movement gained traction, yet it speaks to the same issues of pollution and destruction caused by humans that are still relevant today.

Solidarity economies are quite different from oligarchic economies, but they have one thing in common: both offer opportunities for those who know how to identify and seize them. In one, opportunities are restricted to a few because power and wealth are concentrated in the hands of a few. In the other, opportunities are more widespread because power and wealth are more evenly distributed. In an oligarchic economy, opportunities tend to be few and far between, and those who are not in the top echelon are often left out in the cold. In a solidarity economy, on the other hand, opportunities abound because more people and organizations are working together for the common good. Of course, even in a solidarity economy, there are still winners and losers. But the playing field is more level, and the opportunities are more evenly distributed.

Solidarity Economic Systems Principles and Values

To appreciate the opportunities that a solidarity economy offers, it is necessary to have a good understanding of the principles and values that underpin it. These elements include cooperation, solidarity, sustainability, and social and economic justice.

Cooperation: The solidarity economy is based on the principle of cooperation, which means that individuals and groups work together to achieve a common goal. This contrasts with the individualistic, competitive mindset of the capitalist economy, which pits people against each other in a race to the bottom.

Solidarity: The solidarity economy is also based on the principle of solidarity, which means that members of a community help each other out and look out for each other. This contrasts with the atomistic, self-interested mindset of the capitalist economy, which encourages people to look out for only themselves.

Sustainability: The solidarity economy is based on the principle of sustainability, which means that we use resources in a way that meets the needs of current generations without compromising the ability of future generations to meet their own needs. This contrasts with the extractive, exploitative mindset of the capitalist economy, which sees natural resources as nothing more than commodities to be extracted and consumed.

Social and economic justice: The solidarity economy is based on the principles of social and economic justice, which means that everyone in a community should have access to the resources they need to live a dignified life. This contrasts with the unequal, exploitative nature of the capitalist economy, which concentrates wealth and power in the hands of a few.

The solidarity economy is still in its early stages, and it is constantly evolving. This means that there are always new opportunities emerging. To be successful in the solidarity economy, you need to be able to identify these opportunities and take advantage of them. For example, the principle of cooperation provides opportunities for individuals and groups to work together to create something bigger and better than they could on their own. The principle of solidarity provides opportunities for members of a community to help each other out and look out for each other. And the principle of sustainability provides opportunities for us to use resources in a way that meets the needs of current generations without compromising the ability of future generations to meet their own needs.

What is Value?

In a solidarity economy, opportunities may take many different forms, but all are based on the premise of exchanging value in a way that benefits both parties involved. For example, a cooperative might offer an opportunity to invest in its business, or a social enterprise might offer the chance to partner on a new project. Opportunities in the solidarity economy are often about creating value together, rather than simply making a financial transaction. In order to take advantage of opportunities in the solidarity economy, it is important to be aware of the different types of value that can be exchanged. This includes not only financial value, but also social, environmental, and spiritual value.

Financial Value

This is the most obvious and commonly-understood form of value. In the solidarity economy, financial value can take many different forms, including cash, credit, and barter. Unlike the oligarchic system, financial value in the solidarity economy is typically exchanged in a way that benefits both parties involved. For example, when you buy a product from a cooperative, the money you spend goes directly to the workers who produced the product, rather than being funneled up to a small group of shareholders. When you invest in a social enterprise, the money you put in is used to further the enterprise's social or environmental mission, rather than simply making a profit for investors.

Social Value

Social value is often intangible, but it can be just as important as financial value. In the solidarity economy, social value is created when we exchange goods or services in a way that builds relationships and strengthens our community. For example, when you buy food from a local farmer's market, you are not only getting fresh, healthy food, but you are also supporting your local economy and getting to know your neighbors. When you volunteer your time to help a community garden get started, you are not only making a difference in your community, but you are also gaining new skills and knowledge. Social value is all around us, and it is an important part of the solidarity economy.

Environmental Value

Environmental value is created when we use resources in a way that protects and preserves the environment. In the solidarity economy, environmental value is often exchanged through practices such as organic farming, permaculture, and renewable energy. When we choose to purchase goods and services that have been produced in an environmentally-responsible way, we are supporting a system that is sustainable and regenerative. We are also helping to protect our planet for future generations.

Spiritual Value

Spiritual value is often hard to quantify, but it is nonetheless an important part of the solidarity economy. Spiritual value is created when we exchange goods or services in a way that is meaningful and fulfilling. In the solidarity economy, spiritual value is often exchanged through practices such as fair trade, community-supported agriculture, and local currencies. When we choose to purchase goods and services that have been produced in a way that is consistent with our values, we are supporting a system that is based on compassion and respect. We are also contributing to our own personal growth and development.

The solidarity economy is built on the exchange of all of these different forms of value. When we are attuned to the various forms of value that exist, we can begin to see the many opportunities that are all around us. With this understanding, we can then make the conscious decision to seize these opportunities and put them to use in our own lives. In this chapter, let's explore the concept of value in more depth, and learn how to identify opportunities in the solidarity economy. You'll learn the importance of taking action on these opportunities, and receive tips on how to get started.

Opportunities for Connecting

We live in an era of big-agribusiness and mega-corporate farms. The family farm is all but a thing of the past, and most of our food comes from huge, impersonal industrial operations. Just four companies control more than 80% of the beef-packing industry, and a single company owns more than a third of the pork-processing market. The chicken industry is even more consolidated, with just four companies owning more than 60% of the market. The food system has become so large and complex that it is difficult for consumers to know where their food comes from or how it was produced. This disconnection is one of the reasons why the industrial food system is so destructive. When we are disconnected from our food, we are less likely to care about the quality of what we eat or the welfare of the animals that are being raised for food. We are also less likely to be concerned about the environmental impact of the food system.

The good news is that the industrial food system is beginning to unravel. As more and more people become aware of the problems with the system, they are seeking out alternatives. The demand for organic food is growing, and farmers' markets are becoming more popular. Community-supported agriculture (CSA) programs are on the rise, and more people are choosing to grow their own food. Slow food is an alternative food system that promotes local, sustainable, and humanely produced food. Eco-friendly food options are marketed as an alternative to fast food and preserved traditional regional cuisine. This type of food production encourages farming methods that use local plants, seeds, and livestock to be more sustainable. By supporting slow food businesses, you can help to create a more just and sustainable food system.

These trends present a huge opportunity for those who are interested in connecting with their food. There are many ways to get involved, and there is a role for everyone. You can support your local farmers market, or join a CSA. You can grow your own food or join a community garden. You can participate in food swaps or start a buying club. You can even advocate for change at the policy level. To stay abreast of new opportunities in the solidarity economy, sign up for email lists, join online communities, follow relevant organizations on social media, attend events and conferences, and read books and articles about the solidarity economy. By connecting with others, you can learn about new opportunities as they emerge and be in a position to take advantage of them.

Opportunities for Learning

In our fast-paced, technologically driven world, it is easy to forget the importance of face-to-face interactions. We can order our food online, stream our entertainment, and conduct our business without ever having to leave our homes. While there is certainly value in convenience, we also need human connection. It's all to easy to develop tunnel vision and become focused on our own work and perspectives. Social media can magnify our differences and distort our view of the world. When we only interact with people who share our views, we fail to develop a broader understanding of the world and the issues that we care about. As we have seen our society become increasingly polarized and divided, it is more important than ever to connect with others and learn about their experiences and perspectives. We have more in common than we think, and can grow by learning from each other if we make an effort to connect. Cooperation is one of the hallmarks of the solidarity economy, and it is essential for those who want to build a more just and sustainable world.

Learning opportunities abound in the solidarity economy. You can take classes, participate in workshops and trainings, join study groups, or go on educational trips. If you want to learn about a particular topic, chances are there is an organization that offers educational opportunities on that topic. Food justice, environmental justice, labor rights, cooperative business, social and economic democracy, decolonization, and climate change are just a few of the topics that you can learn about through organizations working in the solidarity economy. When considering educational opportunities, look for programs that are led by people with lived experience. These programs will offer a more nuanced and authentic perspective than those led by academics or experts. They will also provide you with the opportunity to build relationships with people who are passionate about the same issues that you care about. These relationships can provide support, mentorship, and networking opportunities that will be valuable as you continue your journey in the solidarity economy.

Some educational opportunities are offered by universities, but many other types of organizations offer educational programs as well. These include community and worker-owned cooperatives, social justice organizations, and grassroots movements. There are also a growing number of conferences and events that focus on the solidarity economy. These events provide an opportunity to learn about the latest developments in the field, meet like-minded people, and build relationships. The US Solidarity Economy Network holds an annual gathering that brings together people from across the country who are working to build a solidarity economy. There are also regional and state-level gatherings that provide more intimate networking opportunities. Many educational programs in the solidarity economy are offered on a sliding scale or for free. This is in keeping with the principle of solidarity, which values people over profit.

Opportunities for Change

The solidarity economy is more than just an alternative to the capitalist economy. It is a movement for social and economic justice. Those who are involved in the solidarity economy are working to build a more just and sustainable world. The opportunity to make a difference is one of the most compelling reasons to get involved in the solidarity economy. In a world that is increasingly unequal and dominated by corporate interests, it can be easy to feel powerless. The solidarity economy offers a way to take back power and make a difference. The change doesn't have to be big. Every time you support a worker-owned cooperative, buy from a community-supported agriculture program, or invest in a social justice organization, you are voting with your dollar for a different kind of economy. These small choices add up, and they are making a difference. Whether you're looking for personal growth, expert knowledge, a cause to champion, a greater sense of community, a connection to a movement larger than yourself, or simply to do your part in making the world a better place, the solidarity economy can help you achieve any of these goals.

Social and economic justice might mean different things to different people. But at its core, the solidarity economy is about working together to build a more just and sustainable world. It's about creating alternatives to the exploitative and destructive system of capitalism. And it's about putting people and the planet before profits. It is the remedy for the growth of income inequality, environmental degradation, and human rights abuses that are all too common in today's global society. The solidarity economy is a movement for change, and it offers opportunities for everyone to get involved. You don't need to have a lot of money or special skills. You just need to care about making the world a better place.

Opportunities for Financial Gain

The majority of people believe that to amass wealth, you have to be a part of the mainstream economy. However, this simply is not true. There are plenty of ways to build and maintain your wealth through the solidarity economy. Mainstream investing and solidarity economy investing differ in a few key ways. In the solidarity economy:

- The focus is on building relationships rather than making profits.

- The goal is to create value for all parties involved, rather than extracting value from one party.

- There is a focus on the long-term, rather than the short-term.

These differences may seem small, but they can have a big impact on the way that wealth is created and maintained. When you invest in the solidarity economy, you are investing in something that you believe in. You are also building relationships with the people who are involved in the enterprise, which can create opportunities for future collaboration.

As a member of a cooperative, for example, you are not just a customer or an employee. You are an owner, and you have a say in how the business is run. This type of investment can provide you with both financial gain and a sense of satisfaction that comes from knowing that you are part of something larger than yourself. When a family business that has no heirs is sold to a conglomerate, the original owners may receive a large sum of money. But more often than not, the family business is dismantled and the workers are laid off. The community loses a valuable resource, and the family loses its legacy. In contrast, when a family business is sold to a cooperative, the business is kept intact and the workers maintain their jobs. The community retains a valuable resource, and the family maintains its legacy. Converting a family business to an ESOP *(employee stock ownership plan)* is another way to keep the business in the community and ensure that the workers maintain their jobs.

As a small business owner or entrepreneur, you also have the opportunity to build your business in a way that reflects your values. For example, you can choose to source your materials from local and sustainable suppliers. You can also choose to pay your workers a living wage and provide them with benefits such as health insurance and paid time off. These choices will not only make your business more resilient, they will also make it more attractive to customers and employees who are looking for alternatives to the mainstream economy. Entrepreneurship and small business ownership is daunting to some, but it can be incredibly rewarding. Not only do you have the opportunity to make a difference in your community, you also have the opportunity to build something that is truly your own. You don't have to quit your primary job to start a business, but if you have an idea for a business that you are passionate about, you can start small and grow it over time.

We don't have to abandon mainstream economic activity altogether in order to build a more just and sustainable economy. We can engage in both the mainstream economy and the solidarity economy simultaneously. We can participate in the mainstream economy when it makes sense, and we can build alternatives to the mainstream economy when necessary. There are many ways to do this, and each of us will find our own unique path. The important thing is to remember that we have choices. We can choose to support businesses that reflect our values, and we can choose to invest in the solidarity economy. When we make these choices, we are voting with our dollars for the kind of world we want to live in.

Opportunities for Personal Growth

In addition to providing financial opportunities, the solidarity economy also offers opportunities for personal growth. When you get involved in the solidarity economy, you will have the chance to learn new skills, meet new people, and gain a new perspective on the world. One of the most important things that you can learn is how to cooperate with others. In the mainstream economy, competition is often seen as the only way to succeed. In the solidarity economy, cooperation is key. When you cooperate with others, you can pool your resources and create something greater than the sum of its parts. You will also learn how to resolve conflicts constructively. This is an important skill that will serve you well in all areas of your life.

The solidarity economy is also a great place to meet new people. When you get involved in the solidarity economy, you will meet people from all walks of life who are committed to making a difference. You will have the opportunity to learn from their experiences and build relationships that can last a lifetime. The solidarity economy will give you a new perspective on the world. In the mainstream economy, we are often taught to see the world as a zero-sum game. This means that for someone to win, someone else has to lose. In the solidarity economy, we recognize that everyone can benefit when we work together for the common good. When you get involved in the solidarity economy, you will begin to see the world in a new way. You will see that it is possible to create a just and sustainable society.

The Future of Entrepreneurship

Entrepreneurship is the process of establishing a company with little or no financial resources, often involving risk-taking and creativity. The future of entrepreneurship is likely to be shaped by several factors, including technological advances, the global economy, and changing demographics. A confluence of many factors has spurred an increased interest in entrepreneurship. These include a global pandemic, which has led to widespread layoffs and increased economic uncertainty; increasing income inequality and social unrest; and a general awareness of the need for more sustainable, ethical, and purpose-driven businesses. Society is becoming increasingly entrepreneurial. More and more people are recognizing that self-employment offers opportunities for creativity, flexibility, and financial independence. As a result, we are likely to see even more entrepreneurs in the years ahead. Here are a few trends and changes to keep an eye on:

More People Are Becoming Entrepreneurs

The growth of entrepreneurship has been explosive in recent years and this is only set to continue. This trend is being driven by several factors, including technological advancements, which have made it easier than ever to start a business; a desire for greater control over one's work life and income; and the growing popularity of the gig economy. While there are many reasons why people are choosing to become entrepreneurs, one of the most important is that it offers them a way to solve problems that they care about. In a world that is becoming increasingly uncertain, more and more people are looking for ways to make a difference. And entrepreneurship provides an ideal platform for doing so.

More Opportunities for Women and Minorities

Women and minorities are historically underrepresented in the business world, but this is slowly changing. Women are starting businesses at a higher rate than ever before, and minority-owned businesses are also on the rise. As society becomes more entrepreneurial, we can expect to see even more women and minority-owned businesses in the years ahead. Women-owned firms made up only 19.9% of all firms that employed people in the United States in 2018 but their numbers are growing. The number of women-owned firms increased 0.6% from 2017 to 2018. The sectors of the economy with the greatest increase in women and minority ownership include healthcare, education, real estate, and professional services.

The Globalization of Entrepreneurship

Entrepreneurship is the creation of something new, usually with limited resources. This type of pursuit is important to the global economy as it provides opportunities for others. Although some people see globalization as a bad thing because it can lead to increased inequality, there are also many positives to consider. One of the most important is that it allows entrepreneurs to tap into new markets and find new customers. In a globalized world, businesses have access to a much larger pool of potential customers than they did in the past. This is especially important for small businesses and startups, which often have a limited customer base. Globalization and the rise of technology have made it easier than ever to start a business. With access to online tools and international markets, entrepreneurs are no longer limited by geography. We are likely to see more businesses being started by people from all over the world. Industries such as e-commerce, digital marketing, and software development are particularly well suited to a global market.

The Growth of the Sharing Economy

The sharing economy is made up of people who share their goods, services, or time with others. Airbnb is a classic example of a sharing economy company, but many other companies have followed suit, such as TaskRabbit, Lyft, and Zipcar. The sharing economy is likely to continue to grow in the coming years, as it offers a more flexible and affordable way to consume goods and services. Some parts of the sharing economy took a big hit during the pandemic. For example, Airbnb had to lay off a large number of employees, but is expected to rebound as travel restrictions are lifted. But businesses sharing with other businesses are in a position to grow. For example, ShareDesk, a shared workspace provider, has seen an increase in demand from businesses that need to downsize their office space. Companies can improve their profit margins by sharing resources, tangible or otherwise. In other words: they can earn more while spending less and reducing wastefulness.

The Rise of Social Entrepreneurship

A company's brand, growth, and profitability are all affected by its customers, stakeholders, communities, business partners, and employees. Being a *social enterprise* means that a company understands that it is part of an ecosystem and that all of these relationships are important. Social entrepreneurship is a type of business that is focused on solving social or environmental problems. These businesses are driven by a mission to make the world a better place, and they often use innovative business models to achieve their goals. We are likely to see more social entrepreneurs in the future as more people become aware of the need for sustainable and ethical businesses. For example, we are likely to see more businesses focused on solving climate change, providing access to clean water or renewable energy, or creating jobs in disadvantaged communities.

The Increasing Popularity of Micro-businesses

While the past two years were difficult for businesses, with many closing due to the pandemic, some Americans started their online micro-businesses. These businesses are small, often run by a single person with fewer than five employees, and have low overheads. They are often started by people who have been previously unemployed or underemployed. They are often creative businesses, such as design or food businesses, but can be anything from a pet-sitting business to a gardening service. Micro-businesses are appealing because they require less capital to get off the ground and are often more flexible and adaptable than larger businesses. Entrepreneurial micro-business opportunities continue to multiply, both inside the United States and across borders, as a result of improved education levels, internet access, mobile technology integration, declining costs for start-up companies, and improving global competitiveness. Micro-businesses also benefit from greater digital fluency and a more mature e-commerce marketplace that makes website creation easier, marketing simpler, and online sales more straightforward.

The Rise of Impact Investing

Impact investing is a type of investing that seeks to create positive social and environmental impact along with financial returns. While some investors have been making impact investments for decades, the practice has gained traction in recent years as more people have become interested in using their money to make a difference. The global impact investing market is expected to grow from $502 billion in 2019 to $1 trillion by 2025, according to a report from the Global Impact Investing Network. This growth is being driven by several factors, including an increase in sustainable, responsible, and impact-investing assets under management; the development of new impact investment products; and a growing awareness of the potential for impact investing to generate positive social and environmental outcomes. As more and more people become aware of the need for sustainable and ethical businesses, impact investing will become an increasingly important way to support these businesses.

The Increasing Importance of Sustainability in Business

Sustainability is likely to become an even more important consideration for businesses in the future. The need to address climate change, social injustice, and other pressing global issues will require businesses to operate more sustainably. We are already seeing a shift towards sustainable business models, with an emphasis on renewable energy, circular economies, and social impact. This trend is likely to continue as more businesses realize the need to operate in a way that benefits people and the planet. *Doing good* can have a positive impact on how well a company does financially, and this is called the shared-value opportunity. Many businesses have adopted these practices because they realize there's potential profit to be made.

The future of entrepreneurship lies in ethical businesses that focus on solving social and environmental problems. We are seeing a shift towards sustainable business models, and this trend is likely to continue. Impact investing is also becoming an increasingly important way to support these businesses. As awareness of the need for sustainability increases, more businesses will adopt sustainable practices because they realize there's potential profit to be made. Ultimately, the future of entrepreneurship is about making a positive impact on the world.

CHAPTER 11

Respect

Organizing for Change

Aretha Franklin's song *Respect* is an anthem of empowerment and a call for equality. Released in 1967, the song quickly became a rallying cry for the Civil Rights Movement and has since become an international symbol of respect and admiration.

Taking action might begin with a single person, but it can also benefit from the aid of a few dedicated community members. With the appropriate mindset and playbook, a core group of community members may apply the concepts of organizing and building community wealth. Over time, these practices can have a large impact on the social and economic makeup of a region. Organizing for change in the community is a process that takes time, energy, and dedication. It is not a quick fix, but it is an important step in the journey to creating a more just and equitable society. The following are some tips for organizing in the community:

Know your community: It is important to get to know the people in your community and understand their needs. This can be done by talking to people, attending community meetings, and conducting surveys.

Find a community issue that you are passionate about: Once you know the needs of your community, you can begin to identify the issues that you are most passionate about. It is important to choose an issue to which you are willing to dedicate time and energy.

Develop relationships: Building relationships takes time, patience, and effort. It's important to remember that you're not just trying to get people to like you—you're trying to develop relationships that will help you achieve your goals.

Build a team: Organizing is more effective when it is done as a team. As you begin to organize, it is important to find other people who are passionate about the same issue. You can build a team by reaching out to friends, family, and neighbors.

Develop a coalition: Coalitions can be very effective in creating change because they bring together different perspectives and skills. These allies could be individuals, groups, businesses, or other organizations.

Develop a plan: Once you have a team, you can begin to develop a plan of action. This plan should include a goal, a strategy, and a timeline. It is important to be realistic in your planning and to consider the resources that you have available.

Take action: Once you have a plan, it is time to take action. This might include holding community meetings, conducting research, writing letters, and organizing protests.

Knowing Your Community

An important first step is getting to know the people in your community and understanding their needs. If you want to carry out an intervention or build a coalition, it is more likely to be successful if you understand the culture of the community and the relationships among individuals and groups within it. Getting the perspective of people who often don't have a voice in community decisions and politics is important. This includes low-income people, immigrants, and others who are often left out of the community discussion. There are, however, certain people who should be spoken with.

They're the individuals in important jobs or those whose reputation is well-respected by a significant portion of the community or a particular group. These people include local business owners, members of the clergy, heads of local non-profit organizations, medical professionals, teachers, school administrators, police officers, and local politicians.

Some questions you may want to consider when getting to know your community include:

- What are the major issues affecting your community?

- Who are the important people and groups in your community?

- What are the community's strengths?

- What are the community's weaknesses?

- What is the community's history?

- How has the community changed over time?

To work in a community, it is important to understand it. If you do not understand the community, you will not be able to connect with its members or get things done. An essential component of any community assessment, therefore, is to begin by gathering as much information about the community as possible—its physical and geographical features, culture, government, and beliefs. You can learn a lot about a community by combing through existing data, observing, and listening to members. To be successful in your investigation, you need to collect and organize the data in a way that you can refer back to it and update it as needed. This will help create a community description that others can use.

Methods of collecting community information include:

- **Interviews:** You can conduct interviews with key informants in the community to get their perspectives on the issues affecting the community.

- **Questionnaires:** You can design and administer questionnaires to gather data from a large number of people in a short amount of time.

- **Focus groups:** Focus groups are small, informal groups that discuss a particular topic. They can be used to generate ideas, gather information, and test messages.

- **Secondary data:** You can also collect data that has already been collected by others, such as government agencies, non-profit organizations, or research institutes.

Once you have gathered all of this information, you need to organize it in a way that makes sense and is easy to reference. You can do this by creating a community profile. A community profile is a document that contains all of the information you have collected about the community, including its physical features, demographics, economy, culture, and history. The profile should be concise and easy to read, with clear headings and sections. It should also be updated regularly as new information becomes available.

A community profile can be used for several purposes, including:

- **Planning interventions:** A community profile can help you plan interventions by identifying the key issues affecting the community and the people who are most affected by them.

- **Building coalitions:** A community profile can help you build coalitions by identifying the key people and groups in the community and their interests.

- **Evaluating progress:** A community profile can help you evaluate your progress over time by providing a baseline against which to measure changes.

Creating a community profile is just the first step in understanding your community. Once you have created a profile, you need to keep it up to date and use it to guide your work in the community.

Find a Community Issue that You are Passionate About

If you want to make a difference in your community, it is important to find your place in the community and use your talents and abilities to serve others. You can make a difference by becoming a servant leader. Servant leaders are often found in community-based organizations, faith-based organizations, or service-oriented businesses. They are passionate about their work and are dedicated to making a difference in their community. Servant leaders are not born, they are made. Anyone can become a servant leader. All it takes is a commitment to serving others and making a difference in your community.

Whether or not you see yourself as a leader, it is important to remember that everyone can lead and become a servant leader. You don't need to have a title or position to make a difference in your community. You can lead by example, by sharing your knowledge, or by inspiring others to take action. Unlike traditional power-oriented positions commonly found in business or public sector organizations, servant leaders focus on serving the needs of the community. In doing so, they empower community members to reach their full potential and make a positive impact in their community. Characteristics of servant leaders include:

- **Listening:** Servant leaders listen to community members and take their concerns seriously.

- **Inspiring:** They share their vision for the community and inspire others to take action.

- **Connecting:** They build relationships and connect people with resources.

- **Facilitating:** They create opportunities for others to take action.

- **Empowering:** They focus on the needs of community members and help them to reach their full potential.

- **Teaming:** They work collaboratively and value the contributions of others.

Helping others is part of helping yourself

When you make a difference in your community, you are also making a difference in your own life. When you help others, you feel good about yourself and your contribution to the community. Helping others also gives you a sense of purpose and satisfaction. And, as you build relationships with other community members, you will also find that your community becomes a more supportive and enjoyable place to live. There are many ways to make a difference in your community. You can volunteer your time, donate money, or participate in community events. You can also advocate for change by speaking out about the issues that matter to you. Whatever you do, remember that your actions can make a difference.

Listening to others is validating

Validation is recognizing and affirming another person's thoughts, feelings, experiences, and points of view. It is a way of showing respect for another person. When you validate someone, you are acknowledging their thoughts and feelings and showing that you understand their point of view. Listening communicates that you are interested and care about what others have to say. When you listen, you learn about the community and the people in it. You learn about the issues that are important to them and what they are doing to make a difference. Listening also allows you to build relationships and trust. People are more likely to trust and confide in someone who has listened to them. Servant leaders listen to learn.

Inspiring is powerful

Inspiring others is one of the most important things a servant leader can do. When you are inspired by someone, you are motivated to take action. Inspiration is contagious. When you see someone making a difference in the community, it can inspire you to do the same. When you are inspired by a servant leader, you are more likely to take action and make a difference in your community. Being an active listener and showing that you care is among the simplest ways to inspire others. Being enthusiastic and sharing your vision for the community is also inspiring. When you show others that you believe in them and their ability to make a difference, you give them the power to do so. Giving people some well-timed, heartfelt praise and admiration can have a huge impact. Standing by your beliefs and values, despite opposition, is also inspiring. Maintaining a positive outlook in the face of adversity can inspire others to push through their challenges. Being passionate about your mission promotes productivity and helps people commit to a shared vision.

Connecting is multiplying goodness

Servant leaders know that they cannot do everything alone. They rely on the help of others to achieve their goals. By enlisting the help of others, servant leaders can make a greater impact in their communities. When you involve others in your work, you are tapping into a larger pool of knowledge, skills, and resources. When you connect people with information, you are helping them to make informed decisions. Connecting is about sharing resources and knowledge. It is about creating opportunities for collaboration. And it is about building relationships. When you connect people with resources, you are helping them to improve their lives. Connecting people with resources is a form of social justice. Social justice is the fair and just distribution of resources. When you connect people with resources, you are ensuring that everyone has what they need to live a good life. When you connect people with resources, you are also helping to reduce inequality. Reducing inequality is about more than just distributing resources. It is also about ensuring that everyone has the same opportunities to succeed.

Facilitating is creating opportunity

A servant leader is someone who creates opportunities for others. Facilitating is connecting what community members do to what they care about. It is forming a connection between their day-to-day efforts and a greater purpose. When you facilitate, you provide the resources and support that people need to achieve their goals. But, facilitating is about more than just providing resources. It is also about creating an environment where people can thrive. When you facilitate, you create an environment of trust, respect, and collaboration. When you facilitate, you also provide the structure and support that people need to be successful. Facilitating promotes engagement. When you facilitate, people are more likely to be involved in the work. They are also more likely to take ownership of the work. And, they are more likely to be invested in the outcomes.

Empowering is releasing potential

Empowering others is one of the most important things a servant leader can do. When you empower someone, you give them the power to grow and develop, make a difference, and realize their potential. It builds confidence and competence. Empowering others is about more than just giving them the power to act. It is also about supporting them as they take action. Many people underestimate their power. They think that they can't make a difference. They think that their voice doesn't matter. But, when you empower someone, you show them that they do have the power to make a difference. You show them that their voice does matter. Empowering others is an act of faith. It is believing in someone even when they don't believe in themselves. It is supporting them as they take risks and stretch beyond their comfort zone. When you empower others, you are helping them to reach their full potential. Your example can empower others to lead. When you live your values, you inspire others to do the same. When you stand up for what is right, you empower others to do the same. When you take action, you empower others to do the same. Your example can be a powerful tool for change.

Teaming is belonging

Creating community is about more than just building relationships. It is about creating a sense of belonging. It is about creating an environment where people feel safe, respected, and valued. When you work as a team, you are more likely to be successful. You are also more likely to stick with the work, even when it gets tough. The team is the heart of the community and it's where the work gets done. Cohesive teams are more productive, more innovative, and more successful because they tap into the power of diversity. When you work as a team, you can leverage the unique strengths and perspectives of each team member. This diversity of thought leads to better decision-making, more creativity, and more successful outcomes. Currently, too much power is concentrated in the hands of a few. Forming a community team is one way to start to shift this power dynamic.

Once you get to know your community, you can begin to identify the issues that you are most passionate about. It is important to choose an issue to which you are willing to dedicate time and energy. Some things to consider when choosing an issue include:

- **Your values:** What do you believe in? What is important to you?

- **Your skills and abilities:** What are you good at? How can you use your skills to address the issue?

- **Your interests:** What do you enjoy doing? What are you curious about?

- **Your experiences:** What have you experienced in life that has led you to care about this issue?

The issue you choose to focus on will likely be influenced by your values, skills, interests, and experiences. Values that promote community wealth-building include:

- **Equality:** Everyone deserves to be treated fairly, with respect, and with dignity.

- **Diversity:** We are all unique and we all have something to contribute.

- **Inclusion:** We all should have a seat at the table and a voice in the decisions that affect us.

- **Collaboration:** Working together we can achieve more than we can on our own.

- **Empowerment:** We all have the power to make a difference.

Skills and abilities that promote diversity, inclusion, empowerment, and community wealth-building include:

- **Affirming values:** Acknowledging the values that others hold even if they are different from your own.

- **Listening:** Actively hearing what others are saying and respecting their point of view, even if you don't agree with it.

- **Communicating:** Sharing information and ideas clearly, in a way that everyone can understand.

- **Community organizing:** Bringing people together to achieve a common goal.

- **Envisioning goals:** Working with others to create a shared vision for the future.

- **Setting goals:** Working with others to set achievable goals that will move the community forward.

- **Facilitating:** Helping a group to work together effectively towards a common goal.

- **Leading:** Taking on the responsibility to help move a group or an organization forward.

- **Representing:** Serving as a spokesperson for the community.

- **Motivating:** Inspiring yourself and others to take action.

- **Managing:** Keeping people and resources on track to achieve a goal.

- **Collective bargaining:** Negotiating with employers on behalf of a group of workers.

You don't have to have all of these skills to be effective. You just need to be willing to learn and use the skills that you do have to make a difference. And, while these values and skills are important, they are not the only things to consider when choosing an issue. You also need to be realistic about what you can accomplish. When setting your sights too high, you run the risk of getting overwhelmed and discouraged. It is important to choose an issue that you are passionate about, but that is also manageable. Some things to consider when setting your sights:

- **The scope of the issue:** Is this something you can realistically address?

- **Your level of commitment:** How much time and energy are you willing to put into this?

- **Your resources:** Do you have the time, money, and other resources necessary to address the issue?

- **The assets of your community:** What resources does your community have that you can tap into?

- **The needs of your community:** What does your community need to address the issue?

- **The support from others:** Do you have the support of your family, friends, and community?

Your interests and experiences are additional factors to consider when choosing a community issue. If you have experienced discrimination, you may be passionate about working to end discrimination in your community. If you have experienced economic hardship, you may be interested in working to improve the economic conditions in your community. If you have experienced violence, you may be interested in working to end violence in your community.

If you are a person of privilege and have not experienced these things yourself, you can still care about and work to address them. But it is important to check your assumptions and be conscious of the ways that you benefit from inequality. Listen to those who are directly affected because they are the experts on their own experiences. Work to promote the leadership of those who are directly affected because they should be in the driver's seat, leading the way.

Developing Relationships

Once you have a good understanding of your community, you can begin to develop relationships with the people and groups within it. These relationships will be important when you're trying to build a coalition or carry out an intervention. Building relationships takes time, patience, and effort. It's important to remember that you're not just trying to get people to like you—you're trying to develop relationships that will help you achieve your goals. When you're first getting to know someone, it's important to be genuine and authentic. Be yourself and don't try to be someone you're not. As you get to know someone better, you can begin to share more personal information about yourself. It's also important to be a good listener. Listen more than you talk and try to understand the other person's point of view. Show that you're interested in what they have to say and be respectful of their opinions, even if you don't agree with them. It's also important to be dependable and follow through on your commitments. If you say you're going to do something, do it. People will be more likely to trust and respect you if they know you can be counted on. And finally, don't forget to have fun! Spending time with the people in your community should be enjoyable. If it's not, then you're likely to burn out quickly and won't be as effective in achieving your goals.

Building a Team

Organizing is more effective when it is done as a team. As you begin to organize, it is important to find other people who are passionate about the same issue. You can build a team by reaching out to friends, family, and neighbors. It is important to choose an issue to which you and others are willing to dedicate time and energy. Selecting team members who have different skills, abilities, and experiences can also be helpful. You may want to consider forming a steering committee or core group to help make decisions and keep the group organized. Teams function best when they have a clear mission, defined roles, and regular communication. The mission should be specific and focus on a single issue. The roles should be assigned based on the skills and abilities of the team members. And the team should communicate regularly to ensure that everyone is on the same page.

Tips for Creating a Successful Team

- **Choose the right people:** The first step to creating a successful team is to choose the right people. You need to find individuals who are passionate about the same issue, have different skills and abilities, and can communicate effectively.

- **Define the team's mission:** The team should have a clear mission that everyone understands. This will help them stay focused and motivated.

- **Establish norms for how the team will work together:** The team should agree on how they will communicate with each other, how often they will meet, and what the roles of each member are.

- **Give the team a task to complete:** Start the team off by giving them a task that they can complete together. This will help them get used to working together and help them learn how to communicate and cooperate.

- **Monitor the team's progress:** Once the team is up and running, it is important to monitor their progress and give them feedback. This will help them learn from their successes and failures and continue to improve.

- **Recognize and celebrate the team's accomplishments:** Recognize and celebrate the team's accomplishments to help them feel appreciated for their work. This will help them stay motivated and committed to the team.

More than just a group of individuals

A team is more than just a collection of individuals who work together toward a common objective. It's a group that acts as a single unit, pursuing a strong shared vision of success. When working in groups, a cohesive team may achieve more than all of its members working alone because each member's effort supports and complements the others. Creating a team entails selecting the people who will make up that unit, as well as molding them into a functional group. This involves considering how people interact and assisting them in forming group and personal connections. Team building also requires looking at what makes a good team. This includes having a vision that everyone can be passionate about. The next step is to clearly define the idea of a team and make sure everyone understands his or her place in it. After you have the team set up, you need to plan how it will work together. This includes deciding who will do what, how everyone will communicate effectively, and setting norms for the team. Personal issues should be dealt with as soon as possible and resolved thoroughly. Teams need to examine their work and understand the reasons for successes and failures, so they can continue to improve. Team members need to be recognized for their accomplishments to feel appreciated for their work.

What makes a good team?

A good team is composed of individuals who are passionate about the same issue, have different skills and abilities, and can communicate effectively. A good team also has a clear mission, defined roles, and regular communication. It also builds connections and resolves personal issues quickly. Choose the best people you can find to be on your team. They should be a good fit for each other. It is important to think about how each person will get along with the others, and what they will bring to or take away from the team. They should have different skills and backgrounds, but they all need to agree on the team's goal. Competence and humility are important qualities in team members. Each person should be good at what they do but also be willing to learn from others. Flexibility and a growth mindset are also important. The team should be open to change and willing to learn from their mistakes. While they should have a strong drive to achieve, they also should be able to keep their ego in check and not let it get in the way of the team's success. Being able to work together and compromise are essential skills for any team.

The team-building process

The next step in the team-building process is to help the team members get to know each other and build connections. This can be done through team-building exercises or other activities. It is important to make sure that everyone feels like they are a valuable member of the team. Once the team is formed, it is important to clearly define the team's mission and make sure everyone understands his or her role in it. The team should also establish norms for how they will work together. These will help the team function more effectively and efficiently. The team should agree on how they will communicate with each other, how often they will meet, what the meeting times will be, and what the roles of each member are. The team should have a clear vision of what they want to achieve. This will help them stay focused and motivated. Start the team off by giving them a task that they can complete together and will require teamwork. This will help them get used to working together and help them learn how to communicate and cooperate. Once the team is up and running, it is important to monitor their progress and give them feedback. This will help them learn from their successes and failures and continue to improve. Recognize and celebrate the team's accomplishments to help them feel appreciated for their work.

Defining your team's mission

Having a clear Purpose, Vision, Mission, Values, and Measures will help your team understand what you are trying to achieve. This will help them make decisions on their own, instead of always asking someone else for guidance or permission. It will also help you track whether or not your team is achieving its goals, and will help you figure out what is working and what needs to be changed. Your team's purpose is defined as the *why* of your team—why does it exist? For example, your team's purpose could be to *help create inclusive, sustainable, and equitable models of economic success.* Your team's vision is the *what* of your team—what are you trying to achieve? For example, your team's vision could be to *increase the number of employee-owned companies and family businesses.* Your team's mission is the *how* of your team—how will you achieve your vision? For example, your team's mission could be to *start-up social enterprises and promote the conversion of existing businesses to employee ownership.* Your team's values are the guiding principles that inform its decisions. For example, your team's values could be *sustainability, equity, and justice.* Your team's measures are how you will track whether or not you are achieving your goals. Make sure that these are achievable and realistic, so that you can track your team's progress. For example, your team's measures could be *increases in the number of jobs created.*

Giving your team a task

To get your team used to working together and learning how to communicate and cooperate, give them a clearly-defined, short-term task to complete. This could be something like organizing a food drive, planning a team event, or developing educational materials about your team's mission. Make sure that everyone understands their role in the task and that they have the necessary resources. Set a deadline for the task and check in regularly to see how the team is progressing. Creating successful task assignments is a delicate process that requires significant forethought. It's not just about meeting deadlines; it's also about helping employees learn new skills, feel more satisfied with their roles in the organization, build trust between you and them, and ultimately help you refocus on your long-term goals.

Monitoring your team's progress

Monitoring is not the same as micro-managing your team. You should trust your team to do their job and only step in if there are problems. If you find that your team is not meeting your expectations, have a discussion with them to find out why and come up with a plan to improve things. Just like paid staff, volunteers need direction and feedback on how they are doing. They need someone to tell them when they are doing a good job, when things are going well, or if they do not seem to be enjoying a task, what might work better for them. Volunteers need someone to respond to their concerns and give them work or a challenge that is appropriate for their abilities. As your team completes its task, take some time to reflect on their progress. What worked well? What could be improved? What lessons were learned? These reflections will help you continuously improve your team's performance.

Recognizing your team's accomplishments

Showing your appreciation for your team members' contributions regularly, in whatever way you can, will make them feel appreciated and needed. This will encourage them to keep giving their best effort. There are many ways to show your appreciation for your team's hard work. Some ideas include:

- Sending a thank you note or e-mail

- Giving a small gift

- Taking the team out for lunch or dinner

- Hosting a team-building event

- Publicly acknowledging their achievements

- Letting them know about upcoming events or opportunities

- Creating a social media profile or blog post about their work

- Giving them more challenging assignments

- Providing opportunities for them to learn new skills

Investing time to build your volunteer program and taking care of your volunteers can yield great benefits for your organization. A well-run volunteer program can save you money, help you achieve your mission, and make your project more enjoyable. When your volunteers feel appreciated, they are more likely to stick around and continue giving their time and energy to your cause.

Developing a Coalition

A coalition is a group of people or organizations who have joined together to achieve a common goal. Coalitions differ from teams in that they are usually larger and more diverse. Coalitions can be very effective in creating change because they bring together different perspectives and skills. Coalitions can be formed around any issue, but they're often formed to address issues that affect a community as a whole. For example, a coalition might be formed to improve the quality of schools in a community or to reduce crime. Building a successful coalition requires careful planning and coordination. The first step is to identify the issue you want to address and the goals you hope to achieve. Once you've done that, you need to identify potential allies—people or organizations who share your goals. These allies could be individuals, groups, businesses, or other organizations. Once you've identified potential allies, you need to reach out to them and explain your goals. It's important to be clear about what you're trying to achieve and why you think it's important. You also need to explain how the coalition will work and what each member will be expected to do.

Developing a Plan

Creating an action plan can help you turn visions into reality. An action plan explains how your team will achieve its objectives. It includes a list of specific actions, along with the timing and resources required for each one. Your action plan should be specific, realistic, and achievable. This will help you focus your efforts and make the most impact. This plan should also include a goal, a strategy, and a timeline. It is important to be realistic in your planning and to consider the resources that you have available. A good plan will also take into account the potential for opposition and have a contingency plan in place. A good plan should include the following information:

- What actions or changes will occur

- Who will carry out these changes

- When they will take place, and for how long

- Where these changes will take place

- How these changes will be carried out

- Why you are taking these actions

- What resources (*i.e., money, staff*) are needed to carry out these changes

- Who should know what?

Starting with SMART Goals

Starting your planning with SMART goals will increase the chances of reaching the overall goal and gaining momentum by taking a series of smaller, short-term steps. SMART means goals that are specific, measurable, attainable, relevant, and time-based. The best way to set a smart goal is to use the acronym as a guide:

S—Specific: What exactly do you want to achieve? Be as specific as possible. If you're not specific, then you can't measure your progress and you won't be able to tell if you're achieving your goal.

M—Measurable: How will you know if you've achieved your goal? What metric will you use to measure progress? Goals that you can't measure are not smart goals.

A—Achievable: Is your goal realistic and achievable given your current circumstances? This is important because if your goal is not achievable, then you'll get discouraged and you won't be motivated to achieve it.

R—Relevant: Does your goal align with your values and long-term goals? If not, then you're likely to get sidetracked and you won't be motivated to achieve it.

T—Time-bound: When do you want to achieve your goal? What is your deadline? Deadlines provide us with a sense of urgency and they help to keep us on track.

There are several advantages to using SMART goals:

- They force you to be clear and concise about what you want to achieve.

- They hold you accountable for taking actionable steps toward your goal.

- They help you measure progress and stay on track.

- They make your goals more realistic and achievable.

- They keep you motivated and focused on your goal.

- They help you align your goals with your values and long-term objectives.

- They help you set a deadline for achieving your goal.

Taking Action

Once you have a plan, it is time to take action. This might include holding community meetings, conducting research, writing letters, and organizing protests. There are many ways to take action on an issue. Some things you might consider include:

- **Educate yourself and others:** Learn about the issue and share what you have learned with others.

- **Raise awareness:** Organize events or campaigns to raise awareness about the issue.

- **Advocate:** Speak up for those who cannot speak for themselves. Call or write your elected officials and let them know your concerns.

- **Organize:** Bring people together to take collective action on the issue.

- **Volunteer:** Give your time and energy to support a cause or organization working on the issue.

- **Donate:** Give money to support a cause or organization working on the issue.

- **Run for something:** Use your voice and your vote to elect officials who will support your community. Consider running for local office yourself. Even the lowest elected offices can have a big impact on your community.

- **Invest:** Support businesses that are part of the solidarity economy

Making a difference starts with taking action. We all have the power to make a positive change in our communities. The size of the action is not as important as the fact that you are taking action. Change doesn't happen overnight. It takes time, patience, and persistence. But, changes are cumulative, which means that every action you take, no matter how small, is one step closer to achieving your goal. Actions also serve to inspire others to do the same. So, don't be afraid to take that first step. It might just be the start of something great.

CHAPTER 12

Banks of Marble

Your Money Mindset

Banks of Marble by Les Rice is a powerful folk song that speaks to the struggles of workers against economic injustice. Written in 1949, it paints a vivid picture of the exploitation and unfairness faced by those whose wages don't keep up with inflation.

A discussion of how to build community wealth and social change would probably be incomplete without considering the realm of personal finance. It is important to optimize your money mindset if you want to be financially successful. You can do this by adjusting the way you think about money and by taking action to achieve your financial goals. If you have a negative money mindset, start by changing the way you think about money. Begin to see money as a tool that can help you achieve your goals. Take action to achieve your financial goals by educating yourself about money, setting a budget, creating a savings plan, and investing in yourself.

What is Your Money Mindset?

A mindset is a set of attitudes, a frame of mind, or a typical way of thinking. It can also refer to someone's worldview and philosophy of life. A mindset may also be a reflection of a certain group's social or cultural beliefs. When it comes to money, there are two main mindsets: the scarcity mindset and the abundance mindset. It is important to optimize your money mindset if you want to be financially successful.

Scarcity Mindset

The scarcity mindset is the belief that there is not enough money to go around. Money limitations are a fact for many people, yet a scarcity mindset fosters an internal belief system that you will never be able to reach your financial objectives. People who think there is only a limited amount of something *(e.g., job opportunities, money)* feel anxious and insecure. They also tend to focus on what they lack instead of what they have. People who think this way are more likely to hoard money and possessions out of fear they will not have enough. They may also be prone to making impulsive purchases and financial decisions driven by fear or desperation. A scarcity mindset can keep you from achieving your financial goals and can lead to financial problems.

Abundance Mindset

The abundance mindset, on the other hand, is the belief that there is plenty of money to go around. Even though job opportunities and money can be in short supply, people who think this way focus on what they have instead of what they lack. People with an abundance mindset are more confident and optimistic, and also more generous with their time, money, and resources. A positive money mindset is important because it allows you to see the possibilities for creating wealth in your life. It also allows you to take risks and work hard to achieve your financial goals. Having a positive money mindset gives you the confidence to believe in yourself and your ability to create wealth.

Growth Mindset

A growth mindset is a belief that you can get better at things with effort and learning, while a fixed mindset is a belief that you are born with a certain level of talent and that's it. People with a fixed mindset give up more quickly because they don't think they can improve, while people with a growth mindset understand that everyone has room to grow given time and patience. They are more likely to take on challenges and persist in the face of setbacks. A growth mindset is important for financial success because it allows you to see failure as an opportunity to learn and grow. It also allows you to be more open to taking risks, which is essential for wealth creation. Having a growth mindset gives you the confidence to believe in yourself and your ability to create wealth and allows you to see the possibilities for creating wealth in your life.

Optimize Your Money Mindset

It is important to optimize your money mindset if you want to be financially successful. You can do this by adjusting the way you think about money and by taking action to achieve your financial goals. If you have a negative money mindset, start by changing the way you think about money. Begin to see money as a tool that can help you achieve your goals. Start thinking about ways to make more money and ways to save money. Take action to achieve your financial goals by educating yourself about money, setting a budget, creating a savings plan, and investing in yourself.

You can optimize your money mindset by:

- Believing that you can create wealth

- Focusing on what you have instead of what you lack

- Being more confident and optimistic

- Taking risks and persisting in the face of setbacks

- Seeing failure as an opportunity to learn and grow

- Learning about money and how it works

- Changing your money beliefs and patterns

- Making a plan to achieve your financial goals

- Taking action to achieve your financial goals

Identify Your Money Blocks

Money blocks are the beliefs and patterns of thinking that keep you from achieving your financial goals. Some common money blocks include:

- *I'm not good with money.*

- *I don't deserve to be wealthy.*

- *I'm not smart enough to invest.*

- *I don't have time to save money.*

- *I'm not lucky when it comes to money.*

If you want to optimize your money mindset, it is important to identify your money blocks and work to change your thinking. Begin by identifying the money blocks that are holding you back. Once you have identified your money blocks, start working on changing your thinking. Challenge your money blocks by asking yourself why you believe them. Are they really true? If not, what evidence do you have to disprove them?

Even if there is some validity to your money blocks, is there a way to work around them? For example, if you believe you're not good with money, can you take some time to educate yourself about personal finance? If you believe you don't deserve to be wealthy, can you work on changing your mindset and increasing your self-worth? If you believe you're not smart enough to invest, can you begin learning about investing and taking small steps to get started?

Remember, you can change your money mindset and achieve your financial goals. It all starts with changing the way you think about money. After you have challenged your money blocks, start working on replacing them with positive, empowering beliefs about money.

- *Money is a tool that can help me achieve my goals.*

- *I am capable of handling my finances.*

- *I have the time to save and invest money.*

- *I am confident and optimistic about my financial future.*

- *I deserve to be wealthy.*

Start taking action to achieve your financial goals and begin building wealth today. Remember, you are in control of your money mindset. Choose to think positively about money and take action to achieve your goals. You can create the financial future you want. Optimizing your money mindset is the first step.

Educating Yourself About Money

It's more important than ever to be financially literate in today's world. Financial literacy is the ability to understand financial concepts and make informed money decisions. It also means that you understand financial issues everybody deals with like saving money, paying bills, managing debt, investing, and retirement planning.

Financial literacy is a critical life skill that everyone should learn. Unfortunately, many people are not taught about money in school and do not have the financial education they need to make informed money decisions. If you want to optimize your money mindset, start by educating yourself about money.

Learn about personal finance, investing, and economics. The more you know about money, the less mysterious and scary it will seem. When you understand how money works, you will be less likely to make financial mistakes. There are many resources available to help you learn about money. You can read books, listen to podcasts, or take classes. You can also find helpful information online. Whether you take a class or learn on your own, here are the fundamental concepts you should understand:

- Budgeting to manage your money

- Setting financial goals

- Paying bills and saving money

- Managing debt

- Investing for retirement

- Protecting against money schemes and identity theft

It's never too late to learn about money. Whether you're fresh out of school or decades into your career, there's always more to learn about managing your finances. Fortunately, there are plenty of resources available to help you get started. Here are five of the best ways to educate yourself about money.

Read books or articles about personal finance: Start with some basics like budgeting and saving, then move on to more advanced concepts like investing and retirement planning.

Take a class or attend a seminar: Many community colleges offer personal finance courses, and there are also plenty of private organizations that offer seminars on various financial topics.

Meet with a financial advisor: If you want personalized advice on your finances, meeting with a financial advisor is a great option. Financial advisors can help you develop a budget, save for retirement, and make smart investment choices. They can also answer any questions you have about money. Look for a fee-only financial advisor who doesn't receive commissions for selling products; that way, you'll know that their advice is unbiased.

Listen to podcasts or watch videos about money: There are tons of great podcasts and videos about money out there. listening to or watching one *(or two, or three)* is a great way to educate yourself about personal finance in a fun and engaging way.

Use financial planning software: This type of software can help you track your spending, develop a budget, monitor your credit score, and more. Plus, it's a great way to get an overview of your financial situation so you can identify areas where you need to improve.

Learning about money doesn't have to be difficult or boring—there are plenty of ways to make it fun! Try out some of the methods listed above and see which ones work best for you. And before you know it, you'll be an expert on all things personal finance!

Teaching Your Kids About Money

We need to do a better job educating our children about money and business. Our schools are not doing enough of it, so it is up to each of us to pass on what we've learned so that they may achieve greater things with their lives and contribute more value to society in more meaningful ways. It's never too early to start teaching kids about money because the sooner they start learning about money, the better off they will be.

Setting a positive example with your finances and saving as a parent helps your children understand how to be responsible with their own money. When children see their parents making smart decisions with money, they are more likely to do the same. Make sure you are talking to your kids about money often and teaching them the importance of saving for the future.

There are several different things you can do to teach your kids about money. One thing you can do is to give them an allowance. This will help them learn how to save money and how to spend it wisely. Help them understand that they need to be responsible with their spending and that they can't always buy everything they want. This will teach them the value of money and how to budget wisely.

Another thing you can do is to take them shopping with you and let them help you make decisions about what to buy. This will teach them about budgeting and how to do comparison shopping, which is finding the best quality items for the least amount of money. Track your spending for a month to help them understand where the money goes and how quickly it can disappear if they're not careful with their spending.

You can also teach them about investing by opening up a savings account for them and helping them to understand how interest works. Teaching children about delayed rewards, such as saving, is easier when you set reachable objectives. Try using a glass mason jar to help kids see their money grow over time. When they make a deposit, watch the level of cash rise in the container. This will help them understand that saving now can lead to larger amounts of money later.

Warn them about the dangers of debt. Make sure they understand that using credit can lead to high-interest payments and that it's important to only borrow what they can afford to pay back. Help them understand how to use credit wisely. They need to know that borrowing money can be helpful in some cases, but it can also be very dangerous if not used responsibly. Teach them about things like credit cards and loans, and explain how easy it is to get into debt if you're not careful.

You can also start teaching them about entrepreneurship at an early age. Show them how to be creative and come up with ideas for businesses. Help them understand that there are many different ways to make money and that some people choose to work for themselves. This will teach them about financial responsibility and the importance of hard work.

There are many different ways to teach your kids about money, but the most important thing is that you start early. The sooner they start learning about money, the better off they will be. By teaching them about money now, you are setting them up for a bright future. Whatever you do, make sure you are teaching your kids about money in a way that is age-appropriate and that they can understand.

Developing Money Micro-habits

Many people struggle with developing new habits, whether it be quitting smoking, losing weight, getting more organized, saving more money, or investing in themselves. But what if there was a way to make habit development easier?

What if you could break it down into smaller, more manageable tasks? This is where micro-habits come in. Micro-habits are tiny tasks that you can do daily that will eventually lead to larger changes.

For example, if your goal is to learn about managing money, a micro-habit could be reading one article about personal finance each day. Or, if your goal is to save more money, a micro-habit could be setting aside $5 from each paycheck into a savings account.

The key with micro-habits is to make them as small and easy as possible so that you can stick with them. Once they become part of your routine, you can start to slowly increase the difficulty or frequency as you see fit.

The beauty of micro-habits is that they are easy to stick to because they are so small. And, over time, they can lead to big changes. So if you're struggling to develop new habits, try breaking it down into smaller tasks with micro-habits. It might just be the key to success.

One thing to keep in mind with micro-habits is that they should not be something that you have to force yourself to do. They should be something that you enjoy doing or that doesn't take much effort. This way, you are more likely to stick with them.

If you find that a micro-habit is becoming too much of a chore, then it's time to rethink it. The goal is to make it something that you look forward to doing each day. Some micro-habits that can help you develop better money management skills include:

- Tracking your spending for one week

- Saving $5 from each paycheck

- Investing in yourself by taking an online course or reading one book about personal finance each month

- Creating a budget and sticking to it

- Paying off one debt at a time

- Learning about investing and how to grow your money

- Building an emergency fund

- Planning for retirement

- Giving back by donating to a cause you care about or volunteering your time

- Celebrating your successes *(no matter how small)*

You can use micro-habits to help you with any goal, not just financial ones. The key is to find something that works for you and that you can stick with. Once you have developed the habit, you can start to slowly increase the difficulty or frequency as you see fit. And remember, the goal is not to be perfect but to make progress.

Individual Wealth Building

Individual wealth building is the process of creating and accumulating wealth through individual financial and investment activities. The term usually refers to activities such as saving, investing, and budgeting that are undertaken by individuals to secure their financial future.

The best way to build wealth is to start early and make it a habit. The sooner you start saving and investing, the more time your money will have to grow. And the more you can commit to saving and investing, the more wealth you will be able to build.

Everyone's financial situation is different, but there are some tried-and-true methods for building wealth that anyone can use. Whether you're just starting on your journey to financial independence or you're well on your way, these methods can help you build the wealth you desire.

Individual Development Account (IDA)

Individual wealth-building is a community wealth-building approach that aims to increase the savings of low- and moderate-income individuals. One of the pioneering initiatives in this field is the Individual Development Account *(IDA)*. IDAs are an important tool for increasing the savings of low-income individuals and closing the wealth gap. Since they were first introduced in the early 1990s, they have grown in popularity and are now offered by several government agencies, non-profit organizations, and financial institutions.

IDAs are structured as savings accounts, and they are typically matched with funds from private donors, foundations, or government agencies. For every dollar that an IDA account holder saves, they receive an additional matching contribution. The account holder can then use this money to pay for their chosen asset, such as a down payment on a home or the costs of starting a small business.

Savers are normally required to complete financial education courses before they can open an IDA account. These courses help savers learn about topics such as budgeting, saving, and investing. The courses also teach savers how to use their IDA accounts to reach their financial goals. IDAs are long-term savings tools, and account holders typically have between three and five years to save for their chosen asset.

Short-term Planning

Building wealth requires both short-term and long-term planning. In the short term, individuals need to focus on increasing their income and reducing their expenses. This can be done by finding ways to earn more money, such as getting a better-paying job or starting a side hustle, and by cutting back on unnecessary expenses.

Budgeting is an important tool for short-term wealth building. By tracking their income and expenses, individuals can make sure that they are spending less than they earn and redirect any surplus income toward savings and investments. Budgeting tools may include computer spreadsheets, online budgeting apps, or good old-fashioned pen and paper. The key is to capture all sources of income and all expenses so that there is a clear picture of your financial situation.

Determine how much you need to save each month to reach your financial goals. Once you have your budget set up, make sure you automate your savings so that you don't have to think about it each month—this will help you stay disciplined and on track.

Long-term Planning

In the long term, individuals need to invest their money wisely so that it can grow over time. This can be done by investing in assets such as stocks, bonds, and real estate. Individuals can also build wealth by taking advantage of government programs and benefits, such as Social Security and 401(k) plans.

When you invest in stocks, bonds, and mutual funds, you're essentially allowing yourself to make money while you sleep. Of course, there are risks involved with investing, but if done wisely, investing can be a great way to grow your wealth over time.

Make saving for retirement a priority. Saving for retirement may seem like a long way off, but it's never too early or too late to start planning for the future. If your employer offers a 401 *(k)* match, make sure that you're contributing at least enough money each month to take advantage of the match. This is essentially free money that can go towards growing your wealth over time.

Invest in Yourself

This means taking the time to learn about personal finance and investing, and then putting that knowledge into action. The more you know about money, the better equipped you'll be to make wise financial decisions that will help you build wealth over time. There are a variety of resources available to help you learn about personal finance and investing, so there's no excuse not to educate yourself on the subject. Sites like Investopedia and NerdWallet offer a wealth of information on topics like budgeting, saving, and investing, and they're a great place to start if you're not sure where to begin.

Invest in Assets, not Liabilities

An asset is something that puts money in your pocket, such as a rental property or a portfolio of stocks and mutual funds. A liability, on the other hand, is something that costs you money, such as a car payment or a credit card balance. By focusing on investing in assets, you'll be better able to grow your wealth over time. And if you're not sure where to start when it comes to investing in assets, don't worry—there are plenty of resources available to help guide you in the right direction.

Live Below Your Means

This means spending less than you earn and investing the difference wisely. One way to achieve this is by creating a budget and sticking to it. This will help ensure that you're spending less than you're bringing in each month, which will give you more money to invest in assets that will grow your wealth over time. Additionally, living below your means doesn't mean that you have to deprive yourself—it simply means being mindful of your spending and making choices that align with your long-term financial goals.

Start a Side Hustle

In today's gig economy, side hustles are more popular than ever before—and for good reason! A side hustle is a great way to earn some extra cash and grow your wealth over time. If you're not sure where to start, consider Ubering, dog walking, or house cleaning—all easy ways to make some extra cash on the side.

Get Rid of Debt

If you want to get ahead financially, you must focus on paying off debt—especially high-interest debt like credit cards and personal loans. Not only will this save you money in interest payments over time, but it will also free up more money each month that can be put toward savings or investments.

Setting Financial Goals

When you have various objectives for your financial health, it motivates you to take action, be strategic about your spending, and create a plan to achieve those goals. The more financial knowledge you have, the more likely you are to set goals for yourself and become excited about achieving them. You will also be more determined to work towards your goals.

Setting financial goals can be difficult and confusing. There are a lot of things to think about when it comes to your finances. And, everyone's financial goals will be different because everyone's situation is different. But as you work to improve your finances, you must create goals that are realistic and achievable. You need to make a plan that will help you reach your goals.

Money-related objectives or milestones are a form of goal that you establish for your money over time. These goals might be as basic as increasing your savings account balance or planning a holiday. Financial goals are important as it helps give your money purpose and ensure it is going to work for you too. They should be specific, realistic, and have a timeframe. Some examples of financial goals are:

- Save $X amount by X date for a down payment on a house or car

- Have an emergency fund that covers X months of expenses

- Pay off X debt within X years

- Save X percentage of your income each month

- Reach a certain net worth by retirement

- Max out your 401k or another retirement account each year

- Create a budget and stick to it

- Set aside money each month for fun/entertainment/vacations

- Pay bills on time each month

- Build up your credit score

When it comes to financial goal setting, many people focus only on the end goal. But to achieve your goal successfully, it is important to focus on the steps and financial planning needed. This will help you stay on track and achieve your goal. This means figuring out what you need to do and when you need to do it to reach your target. What are three of the most important financial goals?

Preparing for emergencies: Expenses like these might be anything from home repairs to medical bills to job loss, depending on your situation. One of your first financial objectives is to make sure you have a six-month emergency fund set aside.

Paying your debt: The next financial goal you should focus on is paying off your debt, whether that's credit card debt, student loans, or anything else. Unpaid debt is a drain on your finances, and it can be difficult to get ahead when you're making debt payments.

Investing for retirement: Retirement may seem like a long way off, but it's never too early to start saving. Investing for retirement is one of the smartest financial moves you can make. The sooner you start, the more time your money has to grow.

Managing Debt

Debt is money that you owe to someone else. It can be helpful to use debt to finance major purchases like a home or a car. However, it is important to make sure that you can afford to pay back the debt. If you have too much debt, it can lead to financial problems.

Debt involves borrowing money and then paying back more money than you originally borrowed. This is because of something called interest, which is the cost of borrowing money. The higher the interest rate, the more it will cost you to borrow money. This is because you will be paying more money in interest.

It is important to try to pay off debt as quickly as possible so you don't have to pay as much interest. There are a few ways to get out of debt. One way is to make extra payments on your debt each month. Another way is to refinance your debt at a lower interest rate. One way to manage debt is to make a budget and stick to it. This will help you see where your money is going each month and where you can cut back to make debt payments.

Credit Cards

Credit cards can be helpful when used wisely. They can help you build credit, which is important for getting loans in the future. They can also help you make purchases that you may not be able to afford with cash. However, credit cards can also lead to debt if they are not used carefully.

It is important to only charge what you can afford to pay off each month. Otherwise, you will end up paying interest on your credit card balance, which can add up quickly. Another way to use credit cards wisely is to get a rewards credit card. This way, you can earn points for every purchase you make. You can then redeem these points for travel, cash back, or other rewards.

Credit Scores

Credit scores are important for getting loans, credit cards, and other forms of credit. Your credit score is a number that represents your creditworthiness. The higher your credit score, the better your chances of getting approved for loans and credit cards.

There are a few things you can do to improve your credit score. One thing you can do is make sure you make all of your credit card payments on time. Another thing you can do is to keep your credit card balances low. This will help improve your credit utilization ratio, which is one of the factors that determine your credit score. You can also get a copy of your credit report and check it for errors. If you find any errors, you can dispute them and have them removed from your report. This will also help improve your credit score.

Investing for Retirement

Investing money is one of the smartest things that you can do with your money. It allows you to grow your money while taking less risk than gambling or stock market speculation. When you invest, you are essentially putting your money into something that has the potential to grow over time.

Many people think that investing is only for the rich. However, anyone can get started in investing, regardless of how much money they have. The key is to start small and gradually increase your investment portfolio over time. There is no one-size-fits-all approach to personal finance. Everyone's situation is different, so what works for one person may not work for another.

There are many different types of investments, from real estate to stocks and bonds. You can even invest in yourself by taking courses or starting a business. The important thing is to find an investment that you are comfortable with and that you understand. The following are some good investing practices that every investor should know about.

Diversify your investments: One of the most important things that you can do as an investor is to diversify your portfolio. This means spreading your money out across a variety of different investments, instead of putting all of your eggs in one basket. For example, you might invest in stocks, bonds, real estate, and mutual funds. This way, if one of your investments goes sour, you won't lose everything.

Invest for the long term: Another good investing practice is to invest for the long term. This means buying investments that you're comfortable holding onto for years or even decades. Of course, this isn't to say that you should never sell an investment; there will be times when it makes sense to cash out. But in general, it's best to think of investments as something that you're adding to your portfolio for the long haul.

Be patient: Investing can be a volatile business; there will be ups and downs along the way. However, the key is to be patient and ride out the bumps in the road. If you sell every time there's a dip in the market, you're likely to miss out on some big gains further down the line. On the other hand, if you wait patiently for the market to recover from a downturn, you'll be well-positioned to take advantage when things turn around.

CHAPTER 13

If I Were a Rich Man

Protecting Your Money and Identity

If I Were a Rich Man from the classic Broadway play, Fiddler on the Roof, captures the struggle of a Jewish milkman to make ends meet in czarist Russia. It's a reminder to us all that even when life is hard, we can still find joy in our circumstances and hope for better days ahead.

Preserving your assets is essential for creating collective prosperity and individual wealth. Staying vigilant and taking the necessary steps to protect yourself from monetary scams or identity theft is of utmost importance. Some of these schemes are designed to take your money, while others are designed to sell you something that you don't need. It's important to be aware of these schemes so that you can avoid them. Here are some of the most common schemes and scams related to money and identity theft:

Protecting Your Money

Pyramid Schemes

Pyramid schemes are scams that promise big profits for those who get in on the ground floor. The problem is, no real product or service is being sold. The only way to make money is by convincing other people to join the scheme.

Eventually, the pyramid collapses because there are not enough people to keep it going. The first wave of victims loses the most money because they have invested the most into the pyramid. By the time the scheme collapses, most people have lost everything they've put into it. Pyramid schemes are illegal in many countries because they are unfair and deceptive practices that usually end up harming a lot of innocent people.

So, how can you avoid becoming a victim of a pyramid scheme? The best way to avoid becoming a victim of a pyramid scheme is to educate yourself about how they work and what red flags to look out for. Here are some things to keep in mind:

- You should never have to pay anything upfront to join a business venture or receive training. Any reputable company will not charge you anything to become an employee or distributor.

- You should never be pressured into joining something on the spot without being given time to research it first. A legitimate company will not try to force you into anything before giving you all the information you need to make an informed decision.

- Be wary of anyone who tries to downplay the risk involved in investing your money. All investments come with some level of risk, so be sure to do your own research before making any decisions.

- Find out who owns the company and where they are located. It should be easy enough to find this information online if it's a legitimate company. If not, that's a huge red flag!

- Check with your local Better Business Bureau or Consumer Protection Agency to see if there have been any complaints filed against the company.

- Be suspicious of anyone who promises you guaranteed returns on your investment or tells you that you can make a lot of money without doing any work. If it sounds too good to be true, it probably is!

- Use your common sense! If something sounds too good to be true, it probably is. Remember, if something sounds too good to be true, it probably is!

Ponzi Schemes

A Ponzi scheme is a type of investment fraud that involves promising investors high returns on their investment with little or no risk. The funds raised from new investors are then used to pay purported returns to earlier investors. This creates the appearance that the investment is profitable when it actually isn't. Ponzi schemes usually involve investments in products or services that do not exist, or they may involve fake investments with little chance of making any money. For example, in 2012, Bernard Madoff was sentenced to 150 years in prison for running a $64 billion Ponzi scheme in which he promised investors huge returns on investments in fabricated hedge funds.

The best way to avoid being scammed by a Ponzi scheme is to be an informed investor. Know what you're investing in and research the people and companies involved. Be wary of investments that promise high returns with little or no risk, as these are often too good to be true. It's also important to remember that if something sounds too good to be true, it probably is. When in doubt, consult with a financial advisor you trust before making any major investment decisions.

Advance-Fee Scams

Advance-fee scammers typically target small businesses or individuals who are looking for ways to make some quick money. The scammer will usually contact the victim by email or social media, posing as a legitimate businessperson with a lucrative investment opportunity. They'll use fake names, websites, and even stolen logos to make themselves seem credible. Once they've gained the victim's trust, they'll ask for a sum of money upfront to get the ball rolling on the deal—hence the name *advance-fee* scam. They might promise that this initial investment will be returned twofold, threefold, or more once the deal is complete. In reality, however, there is no deal—it's all just a scam designed to steal victims' money. Victims of advance-fee scams often end up losing thousands of dollars. In some cases, they may even be asked to send more money as the *deal* progresses. The scammers will string their victims along as long as they can before eventually disappearing with all of the money.

The best way to avoid being scammed by an advance-fee scammer is simply to be aware that these types of scams exist and to exercise caution when dealing with anyone you don't know online. Remember that if something sounds too good to be true, it probably is. Be especially wary of unsolicited offers or requests for upfront payments—legitimate businesses will never require you to pay anything before you receive goods or services in return. Also, take some time to do your research before doing business with anyone online. Look up their name and company website independently of any links they provide you with in their emails or messages. If their story doesn't check out or if they refuse to answer basic questions about their business, likely they're not legitimate. And finally, never wire money or send cryptocurrency overseas without doing your due diligence first—these types of payment methods are notoriously difficult (*if not impossible*) to get back once they've been sent.

Online Dating Scams

Online dating scams are when scammers use dating sites and apps to trick people into giving them money or their personal information. The most common type of online dating scam is catfishing, which is when someone uses a fake profile to attract victims. Catfishers will often create fake profiles on multiple dating sites and apps, using different names and photos, to cast a wide net. They will then start conversations with their victims, building up trust over time before eventually asking for money or financial information. Another common type of online dating scam is sextortion, which is when someone uses threats or intimidation to get money or sexual favors from a victim. They will often start by gaining the victim's trust before asking for compromising photos or videos. They may then threaten to share these photos or videos with the victim's friends or family unless they are paid off.

The best way to avoid online dating scams is to be vigilant about the information you share on dating sites and apps. Don't give out your personal information, like your full name, home address, or work address, until you know someone really well. Once you have been communicating with someone for a while and you feel comfortable with them, you can start sharing more information about yourself. But even then, be careful not to share anything that could be used to steal your identity or scam you, like your social security number, credit card information, or bank account information. It's also a good idea to do a little research on the person you're talking to before meeting them in person. A simple Google search can often reveal a lot about someone, so you can get a sense of whether or not they're legitimate. If you do end up meeting someone in person, make sure to meet in a public place and tell a friend or family member where you're going. This will help ensure your safety in case anything goes wrong.

Some other things you can do to protect yourself from online dating scams are:

- Use a reputable dating site or app that has security measures in place to protect users' information.

- Do a reverse image search of anyone you meet online before meeting them in person. This will help you see if they are using stolen photos.

- Be wary of anyone who asks for money early on in a relationship. If someone you're *dating* online starts asking for money, they're likely a scammer.

- Trust your gut! If something feels off about someone you meet online, it probably is.

Nigerian Prince Scams

The Nigerian Prince scam is a type of advanced fee fraud. The scammer poses as a wealthy Nigerian prince or other official and promises a large sum of money in exchange for help with transferring funds out of Nigeria. The scammer will often ask for personal information, like your bank account number, to make the transfer. Of course, there is no money to be transferred and the scammer will simply disappear with your hard-earned cash once they have your information. This type of scam is also sometimes called a *419 fraud*, named after the section of the Nigerian criminal code that outlaws it.

The best way is to simply exercise caution and common sense. Be wary of unsolicited emails or social media messages promising large sums of money. Remember that if something sounds too good to be true, it probably is. And never give personal information like your bank account number to someone you don't know and trust.

Employment Scams

Employment scams are when someone poses as a hiring manager or recruiter to take advantage of job seekers. They will often post fake job listings on job boards or contact potential victims directly via email or social media platforms. Once they have made contact, they will try to get personal information from the victim such as their Social Security number or bank account information under the guise of completing a background check or setting up a direct deposit. They may also promise the victim a large sum of money for very little work. In reality, these scammers are just trying to steal the victim's money or identity.

The best way to avoid an employment scam is to be vigilant and do your research. If you're contacted by someone claiming to be a hiring manager or recruiter, make sure that you verify their identity before sharing any personal information with them. You can do this by looking up the company's website and finding the contact information for the HR department. Then, give them a call and ask if they have any record of the person who contacted you.

Lottery and Sweepstakes Scams

Lottery and sweepstakes scams typically follow a similar pattern. The fraudster contacts the victim—usually via email or social media—and tells them that they've won a large sum of money. Often, the scammer will spoof the email address or social media account of a legitimate organization, like a government agency or well-known company, to make the scam seem more believable. To collect their *winnings*, victims are usually instructed to click on a link that takes them to a fake website or are asked to provide personal information, like their Social Security number or bank account number. Once the fraudster has this information, they can use it to commit identity theft or empty the victim's bank account. In some cases, victims are even asked to pay a *processing fee* before they can collect their winnings—which, of course, they never actually receive.

Fortunately, there are some things you can do to protect yourself from these types of scams. First, if you didn't buy a ticket, you can't win the lottery. So if you receive an email or social media message telling you that you've won a cash prize, it's almost certainly a scam. Second, legitimate organizations will never contact people out of the blue and tell them that they've won a contest or lottery that they didn't enter. And finally, never click on links in emails or messages from people you don't know, and never provide personal information like your Social Security number or bank account number unless you're absolutely certain that it's safe to do so.

Fake Charities

A fake charity scam is when a scammer creates a fake charity or impersonates a real charity to collect donations from unsuspecting people. Sadly, these scams are all too common; in 2018 alone, the Federal Trade Commission (*FTC*) received over 2,200 complaints about fake charities. And with donation season upon us, scammers will be working overtime to take advantage of kind-hearted people looking to help others. The best way to avoid giving your money to a fake charity is to do your research before you donate. Here are a few tips:

- Be sure to verify that the charity is registered with the appropriate state agencies and complies with state laws. You can find this information on the National Association of State Charity Officials website.

- Don't give out personal or financial information until you've done your research and are confident that the charity is legitimate.

- Be cautious of charities that spring up overnight in response to current events or natural disasters. This is a common tactic used by scammers.

- Remember that you can always go directly to the source. If you're considering donating to a relief effort for a natural disaster, contact the Red Cross or another reputable organization instead of relying on links sent to you via email or social media.

- Don't let high-pressure tactics rush you into giving. A legitimate charity will be happy to answer your questions and give you time to make a decision.

- Watch out for charities that use names or logos that look similar to well-known organizations but are slightly different. This is known as *brandjacking* and is another common tactic used by scammers.

- Be skeptical if someone contacts you unexpectedly asking for a donation. Unless you have already permitted them to contact you, it's best not to give them any money.

The Pigeon Drop Scam

Pigeon drop scams are a type of fraud in which victims are convinced to withdraw money from their bank account and give it to the criminals to receive a larger sum of money. The scammers usually target elderly people or recent immigrants who may not be familiar with banking in the United States. Pigeon drop scammers typically operate in pairs or groups. One person will approach the victim and strike up a conversation. Once they have gained the victim's trust, the second person will join the conversation and claim to have found a large sum of money. The scammers will then offer to split the money with the victim if they can help them withdraw it from their bank account.

Once the victim agrees, one of the scammers will accompany them to their bank and wait outside while the victim withdraws the money. The other scammer will then meet up with them and pretend to count out their share of the *found* money. In reality, they are counting out a wad of newspaper or Monopoly money. The victim is then given a phone number to call when they get home so that they can arrange to receive their share of the real money. Of course, when they call the number, there is no one there to answer.

The best way to avoid falling prey to a pigeon drop scam is to be aware of how they work and what red flags to look for. If someone you don't know approaches you and starts talking about finding a large sum of money, be suspicious. Also, be wary if they try to hurry you into making a decision or if they ask you to keep the *opportunity* a secret. It's also important not to set aside any personal belongings, like your purse or wallet, when you go to withdraw money from your bank account. Carry everything with you so that the scammers can't sneak off with your wallet while you're inside. Finally, never give your bank account information to anyone unless you trust them implicitly.

Protecting Your Identity

Skimming

Skimming is a type of identity theft that occurs when criminals attach devices to ATMs or credit card readers to steal people's personal information. With this information, they can make unauthorized purchases or withdraw money from your bank account. Skimmers are typically small devices that can be attached to card readers without being noticed. They may be placed over the top of the card reader so that they blend in with the rest of the machine, or they may be placed inside the machine where they are not visible to customers. The devices work by capturing the magnetic stripe data from the cards as they are inserted into the machine. This data can then be used to clone cards and access bank accounts. There are a few things you can do to avoid skimming scams:

- Be aware of your surroundings when using an ATM or paying with a credit card. If something looks unusual about the machine, do not use it and report it to the authorities.

- Cover the keypad with your hand when entering your PIN at an ATM. This will prevent criminals from attaching cameras near the machine to capture people's PINs.

- Monitor your bank statements and credit card statements for any unauthorized charges or withdrawals. If you see something suspicious, report it to your bank or credit card company immediately.

- Never give out your personal information *(including your Social Security number, date of birth, bank account number, etc.)* over the phone or online unless you are certain that you are dealing with a reputable company.

Phishing

Phishing scams typically start with an email or text message. The message might look like it came from your bank, credit card company, or another organization you do business with and contain fake links or attachments. If you click on the link or open the attachment, you might download malware without realizing it. Once the malware is installed on your device, it can collect your personal information, like account numbers and passwords. Or, the message might direct you to a fake website that looks real but is designed to trick you into entering your personal information. Once the cybercriminal has your information, they can use it to commit fraud, like making unauthorized charges on your account or taking out a loan in your name.

While email is the most common way these scams are carried out, scammers also use text messages *(known as smishing)*, phone calls *(vishing)*, and even social media sites *(spear-phishing)*. No matter how the scam starts, the goal is always to get your personal information so the criminals can commit fraud. The best way to protect yourself from phishing scams is to be vigilant about the emails and texts you open and the links you click. Here are some tips from the FTC:

Don't open attachments or click on links in emails or texts unless you know who sent them and why they're sending them to you. If someone wants you to open an attachment or click on a link, call them to confirm that they actually sent it before doing anything else. Hackers often spoof legitimate email addresses, so even if an email appears to come from a familiar sender, don't automatically assume it's legitimate.

Be cautious of any unsolicited messages with urgent requests for personal information—these are almost always scams. For example, if someone claiming to be from your bank asks for your account number or password via email or text message, don't reply—it could be a scammer trying to steal your money. Call the customer service number on your bank statement instead of responding directly to see if there really is an issue with your account that needs attention.

Don't enter personal information on websites unless the URL starts with https:// and there is a padlock icon next to it—this means the site is secure and less likely to be a fake site set up by scammers. You should also make sure anti-virus software is installed on all devices you use to go online and that it's kept up-to-date at all times. This will help protect against malware attacks like phishing scams.

Shoulder Surfing

A shoulder surfing scam is a type of fraud where criminals watch victims enter their sensitive information, such as credit card numbers or bank account passwords, and then use that information to steal their money. These scams can happen anywhere that people use their sensitive information, including ATMs, gas stations, retail stores, and even online. And because all it takes is for the criminal to stand close enough to the victim to see what they're doing, these scams can be very difficult to spot. There are a few simple steps that you can take to avoid shoulder surfing scams:

- Be aware of your surroundings. If you're using an ATM or entering your credit card information online, make sure that there's no one standing too close to you who could be watching what you're doing.

- Use your body to shield your information. If someone is standing too close to you while you're entering your information, hold up a hand or an umbrella so they can't see what you're doing.

- Use a privacy screen protector on your devices. This will make it more difficult for someone to see your screen without being directly in front of it.

- Trust your gut. If something feels off or if you think someone might be trying to scam you, don't hesitate to move away from the situation or ask for help from a nearby store employee or security guard.

Social Engineering

Social engineering is the act of manipulating people into performing actions or divulging confidential information. A social engineering scam can take many forms, but all share the same goal: to trick you into giving up something of value, like your passwords, personal information, or money. The best way to protect yourself from social engineering scams is to be aware of the techniques scammers use and to know what red flags to look for. Below are some common social engineering techniques and red flags to watch out for:

Impersonation: Many social engineering attacks begin with an email or phone call from someone posing as a legitimate person or organization. They may claim to be from your bank, the IRS, or even a friend or family member. Be suspicious of any unsolicited contact from someone claiming to be from a company or organization, especially if they're asking for personal information. If you're unsure whether the person contacting you is legitimate, hang up the phone or delete the email and contact the company directly yourself using a number or email address you know is real.

Urgency: Scammers often try to create a sense of urgency to get you to act quickly without thinking. They may say there's a problem with your account that needs to be fixed immediately or that someone is trying to gain access to your computer. Don't let anyone rush you off the phone or pressure you into giving away your personal information.

Threats: Scammers may also try to scare you into giving them what they want by threatening you with jail time, loss of money, or damage to your computer. Again, don't let anyone bully you into giving away your personal information—hang up the phone or delete the email and report it as spam if necessary.

Freebies: Who doesn't love free stuff? Unfortunately, scammers know this and may use offers of free gifts or prizes as bait for their schemes. Be skeptical of any offer that seems too good to be true—it probably is.

Trojan Horses

A Trojan horse, or Trojan, is a type of malware that is disguised as legitimate software. Trojans can be used to perform a variety of malicious tasks on a victim's computer, including stealing sensitive data, stealing login credentials, and encrypting files for ransom. The term *Trojan* comes from the story of the Trojan War, in which the Greeks used a wooden horse to sneak soldiers into Troy. In the same way, Trojans are used to sneak malicious code onto victims' computers. There are several things you can do to avoid becoming a victim of a Trojan horse scam:

- Only download software from trusted sources. If you're not sure whether a website is trustworthy, do some research before downloading anything from it.

- Be careful when opening email attachments. If you don't know the sender, or if the email seems suspicious, don't open it.

- Keep your antivirus software up to date Antivirus software can detect and remove Trojans, so it's important to have an up-to-date program installed on your computer.

- Don't click on links in unsolicited emails or texts. This is one of the most common ways that Trojans are delivered to victims' computers. If you receive an unsolicited email or text with a link, don't click on it.

- Be cautious when using public Wi-Fi networks. Public Wi-Fi networks are often unsecured, which means that if you connect to one, you may be opening yourself up to attack. When using public Wi-Fi, only connect to networks that you trust, and be sure to use a VPN if possible.

Malware and Spyware

Malware is short for malicious software, and it's any software that's designed to harm your computer or steal your personal information. Spyware is a type of malware that collects your personal data without you knowing it. Scammers use malware and spyware to collect your personal information so they can commit fraud or sell your information to other scammers. They might also use it to hijack your computer so they can use it to attack other computers or spread more malware.

Malware and spyware scams usually start with an email or pop-up message. The message might claim that there's a problem with your computer or that you need to install software to protect yourself from a virus. It might also say that you need to update your software or provide information to verify your account. If you click on the link in the message, you'll be taken to a website that looks legitimate but is actually a scam. The website might ask you to provide personal information, download software, or take some other action that will install malware on your computer. Once the malware is installed, the scammer can do anything they want with your computer, including accessing your personal information, taking control of your webcam, or making it part of a botnet (*a network of computers that can be used to launch attacks on other computers*).

The best way to avoid malware and spyware scams is to be cautious about clicking on links in email messages or pop-up messages. If you're not sure whether a message is from a legitimate source, don't click on any links in the message. You should also only download software from websites that you trust. And if you're ever asked to provide personal information online, make sure you're using a secure website before entering any information. You can tell if a website is secure if the URL starts with *https* instead of *http*. Also, look for a padlock icon next to the URL. If you see both of these things, it means the website is using encryption to protect any information you enter.

If you think you have been a victim of identity theft, you should contact the Federal Trade Commission and file a report. You should also contact your local police department and file a report. Identity theft is a serious crime, and you should take all necessary steps to protect yourself from it. Sign up for one of the credit monitoring services to keep an eye on your credit report. This will help you to catch any fraudulent activity early and stop it before it does too much damage.

CHAPTER 14

We Shall Overcome

Building a Movement and Going Forward

We Shall Overcome by Pete Seeger is an anthem of hope and resilience in the face of adversity, and serves to remind us that we can remain strong in the face of challenges and eventually overcome all obstacles.

We all have the power to make a difference in our communities, both as individuals and collectively. Recognizing and harnessing this personal and collective power is key to creating lasting change. By understanding how our individual actions can contribute to larger movements, we can become more effective agents of transformation. Taking the time to connect with like-minded people and organizations can help us create powerful networks that are capable of making a real impact. It's important to remember that even small actions can have a big effect when they are part of a collective effort. With the right motivation and support, we can all work together to create positive changes in our society.

Understanding Your Collective Purpose

Understanding your *why* is essential for finding purpose and motivation in life. It's the reason why people are passionate about what they do and why they strive to achieve their goals. Knowing your *why* can help you focus on what matters most and give you the drive to make it happen. It can also provide clarity when making decisions and help you stay on track with your goals. By understanding your *why*, you can unlock the benefits of having a clear purpose in life, such as increased productivity, improved relationships, and greater satisfaction. But it goes beyond that; understanding our *why* is key to unlocking our potential for social transformation and community wealth building. When we understand our purpose, we are more likely to take action toward creating positive change in our communities. We become more aware of how our actions affect others, which leads us to think critically about how we can use our resources to benefit those around us. With a clear sense of purpose, we have the power to create a meaningful impact in our lives and the lives of others.

Staying on Track

It can be difficult to stay motivated when faced with obstacles and resistance, but it's important to remember why you began this movement in the first place. Building a strong support network within your community is essential; having people around who understand what you're trying to accomplish and are ready to help can give you the emotional boost you need to keep going when times get tough. Find ways to celebrate each small victory along the way and never forget that your efforts have the power to create real, lasting change.

Community wealth-building activities are important for creating a more equitable and sustainable society. However, it can be difficult to stay motivated when facing resistance from stakeholders. Here are 10 good ways to overcome resistance and stay motivated when working on community wealth-building activities:

Set clear goals: Having a clear idea of what you want to achieve will help you stay focused and motivated. Make sure that your goals are realistic and achievable so that you don't become discouraged by failure.

Communicate the reasons for change: Explain why the changes are necessary and how they will benefit the community in the long run. This will help stakeholders understand why their input is important and motivate them to get involved in the process.

Get excited: Show enthusiasm for the project and let your passion shine through. This will help create an atmosphere of excitement which can be contagious among other stakeholders, motivating them to join in as well.

Make it about your teammates: Focus on how the changes will benefit your employees teammates, rather than just talking about profits or efficiency gains. This will make them feel valued and appreciated, making them more likely to support the project wholeheartedly.

Delegate change: Allow teammates to take ownership of certain aspects of the project, giving them a sense of responsibility which can be very motivating.

Show them data: Provide evidence-based data which shows how successful similar projects have been in other communities or organizations, demonstrating that success is possible if everyone works together towards a common goal.

Remain positive and supportive: A positive attitude is essential when trying to motivate people who may be resistant to change at first glance; remain upbeat even in difficult situations and focus on solutions rather than problems whenever possible.

Listen first, talk second: Take time to listen carefully to any concerns or objections raised by stakeholders before responding; this will show that you value their opinion and make them more likely to accept your point of view in return.

Apply mindfulness: Take time out from your day-to-day tasks every now and then; this can help reduce stress levels which can lead to increased motivation over time as well as improved decision-making skills when dealing with resistance from stakeholders .

Know you're not alone: Remember that many people have faced similar challenges before; seek advice from experienced professionals or look for inspiration online if needed—there's always someone who has gone through something similar and can offer valuable insight into overcoming resistance.

It is important to remember that progress is made through a series of small steps and victories, rather than one large upheaval. This is a marathon, not a sprint. Change takes time, but it is possible, one small step at a time. This is the key to staying on track. One of the most important things to do is to overcome the fear, fatalism, denial, and distractions that weaken your power and keep you from achieving your goals. We can reduce fear and fatalism, and the social controls that keep people in their place, by emphasizing small daily acts of resistance and courage.

Overcoming Challenges

Social progress movements and activists face a variety of challenges in their efforts to make positive change. Here are 10 common issues they must confront:

Lack of resources: Social progress movements often lack the resources necessary to achieve their goals, including financial support, personnel, and access to technology. This can be addressed by fundraising, seeking grants, and forming partnerships with other organizations.

Limited reach: Social progress movements may not have the reach needed to spread awareness about their cause or recruit new members. This can be addressed by utilizing social media platforms and other digital outlets to reach larger audiences.

Opposition: Opponents of social progress movements may attempt to discredit or undermine them through tactics such as misinformation campaigns or legal action. This can be addressed by staying informed on current events related to the movement and responding quickly and effectively when opposition arises.

Burnout: Activists involved in social progress movements may become overwhelmed or exhausted due to the intensity of the work they do and the difficulty in achieving success. This can be addressed by taking breaks, engaging in self-care activities, and seeking out support from peers within the movement.

Political resistance: Governments may resist social progress movements due to ideological differences or fear of losing power if changes are made that would benefit marginalized groups. This can be addressed by engaging in peaceful protests, lobbying elected officials, and utilizing legal channels for making changes when possible.

Discrimination: Social progress activists may face discrimination based on their gender, race/ethnicity, sexual orientation/identity, religion/beliefs, etc., which can impede their ability to make meaningful changes for those who share similar identities or experiences as them. This can be addressed by advocating for anti-discrimination laws at all levels of government and creating safe spaces for marginalized individuals within the movement itself where they feel supported and accepted regardless of the identity markers they possess.

Lack of representation: Social progress movements may lack representation from certain demographics that could provide valuable insight into how best to address certain issues affecting those communities (*e.g., women's rights*). This can be addressed by actively recruiting members from underrepresented groups within the movement itself as well as reaching out to organizations that specialize in advocacy for those demographics.

Media bias: The media often portrays social progress activists in a negative light which can lead to public perception being skewed against them even if their cause is justifiable (*e.g., Black Lives Matter*). This can be addressed by pushing back against biased reporting through letters-to-the-editor campaigns or boycotting outlets that consistently misrepresent activist causes/groups unfairly (*e.g., Fox News*).

Violence: Opponents of social progress movements may resort to violence which puts activists at risk both physically and psychologically (*e.g., Charlottesville rally*). This can be addressed by providing training on non-violent resistance tactics such as civil disobedience as well as having a plan in place should violence occur during protests/rallies (*e.g., de-escalation techniques*).

Lack of unity: Different factions within a single movement may disagree on how best to achieve desired outcomes, which can lead to infighting instead of working together towards a common goal (*e.g., Occupy Wall Street*). This can be addressed by establishing clear guidelines on what is expected from each faction within the movement so everyone is working towards a unified purpose without compromising individual beliefs/values too much (*e.g., consensus decision-making process*).

Focusing on Incremental Change

Incremental social change is an important part of any movement for social justice. It can be difficult to measure tangible progress when pursuing a large-scale goal, but there are ways to track small successes that can help keep people motivated and show them that their efforts are making a difference.

One way to measure incremental progress is by tracking the number of people who have joined the cause. This could include counting the number of people who have signed petitions or attended rallies and protests. By seeing how many people are actively engaging in the movement, it is possible to see that progress is being made, even if it is not immediately visible in other ways.

Another way to measure incremental progress is by tracking changes in public opinion. Surveys and polls can be used to gauge how much support a movement has, as well as how much awareness has been raised about the issue at hand. Seeing shifts in public opinion can be encouraging, as it shows that people's views on the issue are changing and that more people are becoming aware of what's going on.

Finally, measuring tangible progress incrementally can also involve tracking changes in policy or legislation related to the cause. This could include counting how many bills have been passed or how many laws have been changed as a result of the movement's efforts. Seeing concrete results like this can be extremely motivating and help keep people engaged in the long-term fight for social change.

Overall, measuring tangible progress incrementally when pursuing social change movements is an important part of staying motivated and seeing results from one's efforts. Tracking things like changes in public opinion, numbers of supporters, or policy changes can all help show that progress is being made and encourage people to continue fighting for their cause.

Supporting Businesses that Share Your Values

People are using their power as consumers to vote with their wallets by patronizing businesses that align with their values and avoiding those that don't. When we buy products or services from businesses, we're helping those companies succeed. If they're benefitting from systems that maintain poverty, exploit women, contribute to global warming, or any number of other disastrous things, we're helping to maintain those systems. When we avoid buying from businesses that don't share our values, we're sending a message that we don't support them. This is especially effective when it comes to companies that have been in the news for unethical practices.

Every business has employees, operates in a community, maintains a supply chain, impacts the environment, and contributes money to certain causes. By choosing to support an ethical and sustainable business, consumers can help to support a whole chain of social and environmental effects. These effects can include better wages for hourly workers, more minority-owned businesses in the supply chain, more environmentally-friendly shipping practices, and charitable donations to causes that consumers care about.

Consumers are increasingly asking, *Where did this originate? Who created this?* and *Is it better for the environment?* Many companies are realizing that it is not only the morally right thing to do, but it is also good for business to respond to questions from their consumers. The following are some of the ways you can use your consumer power to make a difference:

- Support businesses that share your values

- Avoid businesses that don't share your values

- Educate yourself and others about the power of the wallet

- Speak up and demand change from businesses

- Support movements that are working to create change

You have the power to make a difference with your consumer choices. The number of socially-responsible businesses has greatly increased in recent years as a result of consumer pressure. In 2011, just 15% of the Fortune 500 corporations issued an annual corporate social responsibility document. But that number has flipped, and now over 85% do.

Check out websites like buycott.com, goodguide.com, and ethicalconsumer. org, which provide ratings and information on the social and environmental practices of companies. Look for certifications like Fair Trade, LEED, and Energy Star, which indicate that a product meets certain standards for social and environmental responsibility.

Ask friends and family for recommendations. Search for businesses on social media platforms like Twitter and Facebook. As the number of socially-responsible businesses has increased, so has the number of ways to find them. With a little bit of research, you can find businesses that share your values and support the causes you care about.

Lobbying for Change

Another way to use your power as a consumer is to contact your representatives at all levels of government and let them know what issues are important to you. You can find your representatives' contact information at www.house.gov for the House of Representatives and www.senate.gov for the Senate. Your state and local governments also have websites where you can find contact information for your representatives.

You can also join or support organizations that lobby on behalf of causes you care about. These organizations can provide you with information and resources to help you make your voice heard on the issues you care about. Some examples of these organizations are the ACLU, the NAACP, and Indivisible. These organizations research the issues, draft legislation, and work to influence lawmakers. Many of them also provide opportunities for their members to take action on the issues they care about.

Voting

Voting is one of the most important ways that ordinary people like you and me can make a difference in politics, policy, and ultimately our lives. No matter who you vote for, it's important to get out there and cast your ballot.

Research the candidates in advance, so that you know exactly where they stand on the issues. Make sure you're registered to vote and that you make your voice heard on Election Day. Don't forget to participate in state and local elections. Most of the decisions that affect your daily life are made at the state and local levels, so it's important to make sure your voice is heard there as well.

Unfortunately, only about 60% of the eligible population votes during presidential election years, and about 40% votes during midterm elections. Even fewer participate in local elections. We need to do better. There are a few things we can do to overcome voter apathy. We need to educate people on the importance of voting, make it easier for people to register to vote, make sure they know when and where elections are taking place, and provide more information on the candidates and the issues so that people can make informed decisions when they go to the polls.

We need to get corporate and dark money out of our elections so that people feel like their vote actually matters. We need to institute reforms that make it easier for people to participate in our democracy, like same-day voter registration and automatic voter registration. We need to reform the Electoral College so that everyone's vote is given equal weight. And we need to hold our elected officials accountable when they fail to represent us or act in our best interests.

You may believe that you have little influence over the issues of dark money, voter suppression, and the Electoral College. But, doing something that you can control—being informed, talking to friends and family, getting to the polls, writing and calling your elected representatives, and even running for something—is much better than giving up and doing nothing.

Voter turnout has been shown to have an impact on public policy. Elected officials respond to those who show up and cast a vote. If wealthier people vote more often than poorer people, the wealthier people will have more of an impact on public policy. The same is true for any special interest group or segment of the population. That's why everyone needs to make their voice heard and continue to press for reforms to level the playing field.

Using Social Media Power

Everyone has some power to effect change on a personal and community level. It may not be a lot, but it's something. And if enough people use their power, they can make a real difference. We can send a powerful message by refusing to tolerate the abuses of power, speaking out, and voting with our wallets for businesses and politicians that are fighting for change. With enough people doing this, we may create a loud voice that says we will no longer accept their tyranny.

Consumers are becoming more aware that they may use social media to create movements around shared principles and bring about change. For example, the *Me Too* movement started as a way for women to share their experiences of sexual harassment and assault, but it quickly grew into a much larger movement that is now sparking change on a global scale.

Hashtag campaigns, such as *#GrabYourWallet* and *#DeleteUber* have also been effective in holding businesses accountable for their actions. The *Occupy* movement was a global protest against economic inequality that began in the United States in September of 2011. The protesters camped out in public places, such as parks and financial districts, to raise awareness of the issue and to demand change. The movement quickly spread to other countries, and while it didn't achieve all of its goals, it did succeed in shining a light on the problem of economic inequality and bringing people together to demand change.

Social media has become an incredibly powerful tool for creating social change. It has been used to successfully organize movements around a range of issues, from living wages and hiring practices to discrimination, workplace conditions, employee unions, and environmental concerns. Social media provides a platform for people to come together and share their stories, experiences, and opinions to create meaningful dialogue. This dialogue can then be used to create real-world action that can bring about positive change. Additionally, social media allows activists to reach a wider audience than ever before, allowing them to spread awareness of their cause and gain support from all corners of the globe.

Modeling Successful Movements

Our society has seen a surge of social progress movements that have changed the world for the better. The secret behind these successful social progress movements is that they are driven by passionate leaders who are committed to creating positive change in society through grassroots organizing efforts such as protests, campaigns, petitions, and other activities, combined with effective communication strategies such as media outreach or online platforms like social media sites or blogs which help spread their message far and wide quickly. Additionally, many of these movements have been able to garner widespread support from individuals, organizations, celebrities, politicians, and other influencers, which helps them gain even more traction.

Anti-Racism Movements: These movements have taken many forms over recent years including Black Lives Matter, Indigenous People's Day celebrations, anti-racism protests, and more. The Anti-Racism Movements have been successful at raising awareness about systemic racism within our society, pushing governments around the world towards creating policies that address racial inequities, and inspiring people everywhere to become allies against racism.

The Fight for $15: This movement, which began in 2012, was a fight for a living wage for all workers. It successfully raised the minimum wage in many states across the country and has helped millions of people make ends meet.

Climate Change Activism: This movement began with grassroots efforts such as Earth Day protests, but has since grown into a global phenomenon with millions of people around the world taking part in climate change activism every day through marches, rallies, petitions, boycotts, and more. The Climate Change Activism Movement has been successful at raising awareness about this critical issue and pushing governments around the world to take action on reducing emissions and transitioning away from fossil fuels towards renewable energy sources like solar power or wind energy.

Schools Strike for Climate: This youth-led movement began in 2018 when Swedish student Greta Thunberg started skipping school every Friday to protest government inaction on climate change. The movement has since spread across the globe, inspiring millions of young people to take action on climate change.

Indigenous Land Rights: This movement seeks to protect and promote Indigenous land rights around the world, from Canada to Australia and beyond. It is focused on restoring traditional land rights, protecting sacred sites, and ensuring Indigenous communities have access to their ancestral lands.

Women's March and #MeToo: These two movements both started in 2017 as a way to fight back against sexism and gender discrimination. They have had an incredible impact on raising awareness about gender-based violence and inequalities, as well as inspiring women around the world to stand up for their rights.

LGBTQ+ Rights Movement: This movement started decades ago but gained momentum over recent years with more people becoming vocal about their support for equal rights regardless of sexual orientation or gender identity/expression. The LGBTQ+ Rights Movement has been successful at passing laws that protect LGBTQ+ individuals from discrimination based on their identity, as well as making strides towards marriage equality.

Treatment Action Campaign: This South African social movement was founded in 1998 to secure access to life-saving HIV/AIDS treatments for all South Africans living with HIV/AIDS. Through advocacy efforts, they successfully secured access to antiretroviral drugs for all those who needed them by 2003.

Tenants' Rights: This movement began in 2014 when tenants across the country organized together to fight back against unfair housing practices such as rent hikes, evictions without cause, and lack of maintenance by landlords. The Tenants' Rights Movement has been successful in passing legislation that protects renters from exploitation by landlords, as well as providing them with more rights when it comes to renting an apartment or house.

Umbrella Movement: This pro-democracy civil disobedience campaign took place in Hong Kong from 2014–2015 as a response to proposed electoral reforms that would limit citizens' right to vote for their leaders freely and fairly. After 79 days of protests, it ended without achieving its goals but inspired other pro-democracy movements around the world such as Occupy Central with Love and Peace (*2014*) in Taiwan and Yellow Vests (*2018*) in France among others.

Gun Control Advocacy: This movement began after several mass shootings occurred across America over recent years, sparking outrage among citizens who wanted stricter gun control laws. The Gun Control Advocacy Movement has been successful at passing legislation that limits access to firearms, such as universal background checks, waiting periods, age restrictions, etc., while also working towards closing loopholes that allow certain individuals access to guns even if they shouldn't be able.

Via Campesina: This international peasant movement is dedicated to promoting food sovereignty worldwide by advocating for small-scale sustainable agriculture that respects local cultures, traditions, biodiversity, labor rights, human rights, and environmental protection principles.

Changing the Course of History

When people unite and work together for a common cause, they harness the power of collective action in a divided world. Movements have changed the course of history. The American Revolution, the civil rights movement, the women's suffrage movement, the LGBTQ rights movement, and the environmental movement are just a few examples.

It's important to remember that progress is not always linear. There will be setbacks but, if we keep pushing, eventually we will see progress. The key is to never give up. Movements work like rivers that persistently change the landscape, eventually carving out canyons and valleys. It takes time, but eventually, the rivers will have a profound impact. Movements, like rivers, need a constant flow of people and action to keep moving forward.

Being part of a movement is contributing to a larger calling that touches on something fundamental in all of us. There is strength in numbers, and when we stand together, we are more likely to be heard and to effect change. If you're feeling disaffected and alone, remember that you are not alone. Others feel the same way and are fighting for the same things. The key is connecting with others, developing a shared purpose, getting organized, creating a plan of action, and sticking with it.

CONCLUSION

Inspiring Quotes from Champions of Progressive Social Change

We all need a bit of motivation and inspiration in our lives, and there's no better source than champions of progressive social change. From Martin Luther King Jr. and Theodore Roosevelt to Margaret Mead and Mother Teresa, these inspirational quotes can help instill within us the courage and dedication needed to make a positive change in the world.

Whether it's about creating something meaningful or just striving for success, these quotes will give you the confidence and willpower to stand up for what you believe in. We have the power to build a sustainable future if we work together towards this common goal.

It is my hope that together we can create a world where everyone has access to opportunity and resources to thrive. So, take some time to peruse through the words of wisdom from some of the most renowned leaders of all time!

> *Never doubt that a small group of thoughtful, committed citizens can change the world; indeed, it's the only thing that ever has.*
>
> —Margaret Mead

> *The most common way people give up their power is by thinking they don't have any.*
>
> —Alice Walker

Injustice anywhere is a threat to justice everywhere.

—Martin Luther King Jr

The only way to make meaningful social change is through collective action.

—Gloria Steinem

I alone cannot change the world, but I can cast a stone across the waters to create many ripples.

—Mother Teresa

Change will not come if we wait for some other person or some other time. We are the ones we've been waiting for. We are the change that we seek.

—Barack Obama

A great democracy has got to be progressive or it will soon cease to be great or a democracy.

—Theodore Roosevelt

Those of us who have in our history the commonality of suffering from hate, we know that those who won the day are those who chose love in the midst of hate.

—Rev. Dr. William J. Barber II

A society grows great when old men plant trees whose shade they know they shall never sit in.

—Greek Proverb

Be the change you wish to see in the world.

—Mahatma Gandhi

Action is the foundational key to all success.

—Pablo Picasso

Progress is impossible without change, and those who cannot change their minds cannot change anything.

—George Bernard Shaw

The only way to make sense out of change is to plunge into it, move with it, and join the dance.

—Alan Watts

The greatest danger for most of us is not that our aim is too high and we miss it, but that it is too low and we reach it.

—Michelangelo

It always seems impossible until its done.

—Nelson Mandela

A journey of a thousand miles begins with a single step.

—Lao Tzu

BIBLIOGRAPHY

350.org. *About 350.* October 5, 2022. https://350.org/about/.

ARISE Adelante. *Home Page.* Accessed February 18, 2023. https://www.arisesotex.org.

Be Freedom. *Principles of Organizing.* October 27, 2018. https://befreedom.co/on-organizing/.

Board of Governors of the Federal Reserve System. *Financial Accounts of the United States - Z.1.* December 9, 2022. https://www.federalreserve.gov/releases/z1/current/.

Brown, Ellen. *How America Became an Oligarchy.* Resilience, December 15, 2020. https://www.resilience.org/stories/2015-04-07/how-america-became-an-oligarchy/.

Bureau of Labor Statistics. *Inflation Rate between 1975-2020 | Inflation Calculator.* Accessed February 18, 2023. https://www.officialdata.org/1975-dollars-in-2020?amount=50.

Business Insider. *21 Ways Rich People Think Differently than the Average Person.* October 22, 2015. https://www.businessinsider.com/how-rich-people-think-differently-2015-8?international=true&r=US&IR=T.

Buycott App. *Buycott.* Accessed February 18, 2023. https://www.buycott.com/.

Cambridge University Press. *Testing Theories of American Politics: Elites, Interest Groups, and Average Citizens.* September 18, 2014. https://www.cambridge.org/core/journals/perspectives-on-politics/article/testing-theories-of-american-politics-elites-interest-groups-and-average-citizens/62327F513959D0A304D4893B382B992B.

Census Bureau QuickFacts. *U.S. Census Bureau QuickFacts: United States.* Accessed February 18, 2023. https://www.census.gov/quickfacts/fact/table/US/PST045222.

Climate Justice Alliance. *Home Page.* February 8, 2023. https://climatejusticealliance.org/.

Coalition on Human Needs. *Home Page.* February 17, 2023. https://www.chn.org/.

Community Development Corporation of Long Island, Inc. *Home Page.* Accessed February 18, 2023. https://www.cdcli.org/

Community-Wealth.org. *Home Page.* Accessed February 18, 2023. https://community-wealth.org.

Congressional Research Service. *How Climate Change May Affect the U.S. Economy.* April 4, 2022. https://crsreports.congress.gov/product/pdf/R/R47063.

Congressional Research Service. *The U.S. Income Distribution: Trends and Issues.* January 13, 2021. https://sgp.fas.org/crs/misc/R44705.pdf.

Consumer Advice. *Scams.* November 10, 2021. https://consumer.ftc.gov/scams.

Consumer Advice. *What To Know About Cryptocurrency and Scams.* May 19, 2022. https://consumer.ftc.gov/articles/what-know-about-cryptocurrency-and-scams.

Cooperation Jackson. *Home Page.* Accessed February 18, 2023. https://cooperationjackson.org/.

CRF USA. *Home Page*. May 12, 2021. https://crfusa.com/.

Deadline. *Politically Divided America Is Very Good For Our Business, Sinclair Broadcast CEO Says*. Accessed February 18, 2023. "https://deadline.com/2022/05/political-division-midterm-elections-primaried-jd-vance-sinclair-broadcast-1235028187/.

Dudley Street Neighborhood Initiative. *Home Page*. Accessed February 18, 2023. https://www.dsni.org/.

Economic Policy Institute. *CEO Compensation Has Grown 940% since 1978: Typical Worker Compensation Has Risen Only 12% during That Time*. Accessed February 18, 2023. https://www.epi.org/publication/ceo-compensation-2018/.

Economic Policy Institute. *State of Working America Wages 2019: A Story of Slow, Uneven, and Unequal Wage Growth over the Last 40 Years*. Accessed February 18, 2023. https://www.epi.org/publication/swa-wages-2019/.

Equal Rights Advocates. *Home Page*. November 11, 2022. https://www.equalrights.org/.

Equity Trust. *Changing the Way We Think about and Hold Property*. December 14, 2018. https://equitytrust.org/.

Ethical Consumer. *Home Page*. Accessed February 18, 2023. https://www.ethicalconsumer.org/.

Evergreen Cooperatives. *Home Page*. Accessed February 18, 2023. https://www.evgoh.com/.

FairVote. *Voter Turnout*. December 16, 2022. https://www.fairvote.org/resources/voter-turnout/.

Fast Company. *Your favorite childhood book perpetuates the meritocracy myth. Three Little Engines sets the record straight*. July 9, 2021. https://www.fastcompany.com/90653350/your-favorite-childhood-book-perpetuates-the-meritocracy-myth-three-little-engines-sets-the-record-straight.

Federal Reserve Bank of Kansas City. *The Past, Present and Future of Black Wall Street.* May 26, 2021. https://www.kansascityfed.org/oklahomacity/oklahoma-economist/oklahoma-economist-the-past-present-and-future-of-black-wall-street/.

Federal Trade Commission. *Report Fraud.* Accessed February 18, 2023. https://reportfraud.ftc.gov.

Foundation Communities. *Home Page.* February 14, 2023. https://foundcom.org/.

Gornick, Janet. *The U.S. Middle Class Isn't Shrinking, But It Is Getting Squeezed as Inequality Rises.* Stone Center on Socio-Economic Inequality, June 4, 2020. https://stonecenter.gc.cuny.edu/the-u-s-middle-class-isnt-shrinking-but-it-is-getting-squeezed-as-inequality-rises/.

Harvard Business Review. *How to Build Wealth When You Don't Come from Money.* March 22, 2022. https://hbr.org/2022/03/how-to-build-wealth-when-you-dont-come-from-money.

Higdon, Nolan. *Media Gets It Wrong on Elon Musk and Twitter: The Issue Is Oligarchy, Not Free Speech.* Salon, April 23, 2022. https://www.salon.com/2022/04/23/media-gets-it-on-elon-musk-and-twitter-the-issue-is-oligarchy-not-free-speech/.

Horowitz, Juliana Menasce, Ruth Igielnik, and Rakesh Kochhar *1. Trends in Income and Wealth Inequality.* Pew Research Center's Social & Demographic Trends Project, August 17, 2020. https://www.pewresearch.org/social-trends/2020/01/09/trends-in-income-and-wealth-inequality/.

ICA Group. *Home Page.* April 11, 2022. https://icagroup.org/.

Immigration Equality. *Home Page.* February 1, 2023. https://immigrationequality.org/.

Indigenous Environmental Network. *Respecting and Adhering to Indigenous Knowledge and Natural Law.* Accessed February 18, 2023. https://www.ienearth.org/.

Inequality.org. *Income Inequality.* December 22, 2022. https://inequality.org/facts/income-inequality/.

Innocence Project. *Innocence Project—Help Us Put an End to Wrongful Convictions!* February 8, 2023. https://innocenceproject.org/.

Investopedia. *America's Middle Class Is Losing Ground Financially.* September 30, 2021. https://www.investopedia.com/insights/americas-slowly-disappearing-middle-class/.

Investopedia. *What Is the Average Net Worth of the Top 1%?* January 10, 2023. https://www.investopedia.com/financial-edge/1212/average-net-worth-of-the-1.aspx.

Karma, Roge. *The Meritocracy Trap, Explained.* Vox, October 24, 2019. https://www.vox.com/policy-and-politics/2019/10/24/20919030/meritocracy-book-daniel-markovits-inequality-rich.

Kellogg Insight. *Why Are U.S. Companies Hoarding So Much Cash?* April 29, 2022. https://insight.kellogg.northwestern.edu/article/companies-hoarding-cash.

Kochhar, Rakesh, and Stella Sechopoulos. *How the American Middle Class Has Changed in the Past Five Decades.* Pew Research Center, April 21, 2022. https://www.pewresearch.org/fact-tank/2022/04/20/how-the-american-middle-class-has-changed-in-the-past-five-decades/.

Kunsman, Todd. *8 Simple Ways You Can Become Financially Literate On Your Own.* Invested Wallet, May 6, 2022. https://investedwallet.com/become-financially-literate/.

Leonhardt, Megan. *Here's who is considered middle-class—and how they fared during the first year of the pandemic.* Yahoo!. April 20, 2022. https://www.yahoo.com/video/considered-middle-class-fared-during-140100983.

html.

M4BL. *Home Page*. August 25, 2022. https://m4bl.org/.

Markovits, Daniel. *Five Myths about Meritocracy*. Washington Post, September 13, 2019. https://www.washingtonpost.com/outlook/five-myths/five-myths-about-meritocracy/2019/09/13/4d90d244-d4cd-11e9-9610-fb56c5522e1c_story.html.

Meserve, Jack. *Countering Nationalist Oligarchy*. Democracy Journal, December 11, 2018. https://democracyjournal.org/magazine/51/countering-nationalist-oligarchy/.

Movement Strategy Center. *Home Page*. Accessed February 18, 2023. https://movementstrategy.org/.

National Domestic Workers Alliance. *Home Page*. February 15, 2023. https://www.domesticworkers.org/.

National Housing Trust. *Home Page*. Accessed February 18, 2023. https://nationalhousingtrust.org/.

Nayak, Bhabani Shankar. *The Oligarchs of Mass Media and the Antidote*. The Citizen. August 25, 2020. https://www.thecitizen.in/index.php/en/NewsDetail/index/4/19261/The-Oligarchs-of-Mass-Media--.

New Communities, Inc. *Home Page*. Accessed February 18, 2023. https://www.newcommunitiesinc.com/.

New Economy Coalition. *Home Page*. February 7, 2023. https://neweconomy.net/.

New Era Community Connection. *Home Page*. Accessed February 18, 2023. https://www.neweraworld.work/

News Literacy Project. *Frequently Asked Questions*. January 10, 2023. https://newslit.org/faq/.

Open Secrets. *Home Page*. Accessed February 18, 2023. https://www.opensecrets.org/.

Oxfam. *Extreme Wealth is Not Merited*. Accessed February 18, 2023. https://www-cdn.oxfam.org/s3fs-public/file_attachments/dp-extreme-wealth-is-not-merited-241115-en.pdf.

Park Slope Food Coop. *Home Page*. Accessed February 18, 2023. https://www.foodcoop.com/.

Partners for Dignity and Rights. *Home Page*. Accessed February 18, 2023. https://dignityandrights.org/

People's Action. *Campaigns*. Accessed February 18, 2023. https://peoplesaction.org/campaigns/.

Philanthropy News Digest. *Billionaire philanthropy is a PR scam, wealth tax proponent argues*. Accessed February 18, 2023. https://philanthropynewsdigest.org/news/billionaire-philanthropy-is-a-pr-scam-wealth-tax-proponent-argues.

Pike Place Market. *Home Page*. Accessed February 18, 2023. https://www.pikeplacemarket.org/.

Poor People's Campaign. *Home Page*. Accessed February 18, 2023. https://www.poorpeoplescampaign.org/.

PowerSwitch Action. *The Partnership for Working Families is now PowerSwitch Action*. Accessed February 18, 2023. https://www.powerswitchaction.org/partnership-for-working-families-is-now-powerswitch-action.

Preserve. *Vote With Your Wallet: Consumer Power as Activism—B The Change*. Medium, December 14, 2021. https://bthechange.com/vote-with-your-wallet-consumer-power-as-activism-4a1c479e09aa.

Recology. *Recology - Compost, Recycling, & Landfill - Collection & Processing*. Recology, June 29, 2022. https://www.recology.com/.

Reeves, Richard V., Katherine Guyot, and Eleanor Krause. *Defining the Middle Class: Cash, Credentials, or Culture?* Brookings, March 9, 2022. https://www.brookings.edu/research/defining-the-middle-class-cash-credentials-or-culture/.

Reich, Robert. *What is Oligarchy?* Accessed February 18, 2023. https://robertreich.org/post/185209385250.

RepresentUs. *The U.S. Is an Oligarchy? The Research, Explained.* Accessed February 18, 2023. https://act.represent.us/sign/usa-oligarchy-research-explained/.

Restaurant Opportunities Center United. *Home Page.* Accessed February 18, 2023. https://rocunited.org/.

Right to the City. *Home Page.* Accessed February 18, 2023. https://www.righttothecity.org/.

Rosenberg, Eli. *What We Know about the Conservative Media Giant Sinclair.* Chicago Tribune, December 14, 2018. https://www.chicagotribune.com/business/ct-biz-who-is-sinclair-broadcast-group-20180403-story.html.

Southern Partners Fund. *Home Page.* February 14, 2023. https://southernpartnersfund.org/.

Spacey, John. *9 Examples of a Meritocracy.* Simplicable. November 18, 2017. https://simplicable.com/new/meritocracy.

Sunrise Movement. *Sunrise Movement—We Are The Climate Revolution.* December 14, 2022. https://www.sunrisemovement.org/.

The Balance. *Does Trickle-Down Economics Work?* December 31, 2021. https://www.thebalancemoney.com:443/trickle-down-economics-theory-effect-does-it-work-3305572.

The Balance. *What Is Middle-Class Income?* December 31, 2021. https://www.thebalancemoney.com:443/definition-of-middle-class-income-4126870.

The Balance. *What Is the Average Income in the United States?* April 4, 2022. https://www.thebalancemoney.com:443/what-is-average-income-in-usa-family-household-history-3306189.

The Center for Popular Democracy. *Home Page.* Accessed February 18, 2023. https://www.populardemocracy.org/.

The Federation of Southern Cooperatives | Land Assistance Fund. *Home Page.* Accessed February 18, 2023. https://www.federation.coop/.

The LAMP. *A Guide to Understanding the News and Making Good Choices.* June 14, 2015. https://thelamp.org/portfolio/a-guide-to-understanding-the-news-and-making-good-choices/.

The Nation. *Ten Things to Start a Movement.* June 29, 2015. https://www.thenation.com/article/archive/ten-things-start-movement/.

The University of Kansas. *Community Tool Box.* Accessed February 18, 2023. https://ctb.ku.edu/en.

ThoughtCo. *Understanding Meritocracy From a Sociological Perspective.* June 23, 2019. https://www.thoughtco.com/meritocracy-definition-3026409.

TRT World. *Viral inequality: Billionaires gained $3.9tn, workers lost $3.7tn in 2020.* January 28, 2021. https://www.trtworld.com/magazine/viral-inequality-billionaires-gained-3-9tn-workers-lost-3-7tn-in-2020-43674.

United We Dream. *United We Dream | The Largest Immigrant Youth-Led Network.* September 15, 2022. https://unitedwedream.org/.

USA.Gov. *Common Scams and Frauds.* Accessed February 19, 2023. https://www.usa.gov/common-scams-frauds.

U.S. Bureau of Labor Statistics. *CPI Inflation Calculator.* Accessed February

18, 2023. https://data.bls.gov/cgi-bin/cpicalc.pl?cost1=9,870.00.

U.S. Bureau of Labor Statistics. *Inflation Calculator.* Accessed February 18, 2023. https://www.bls.gov/data/inflation_calculator.htm.

U.S. Census Bureau. *Historical Income Tables: Households.* Census.gov, August 18, 2022. https://www.census.gov/data/tables/time-series/demo/income-poverty/historical-income-households.html.

U.S. Census Bureau. *Income in 1970 of Families and Persons in the United States.* Census.gov, October 8, 2021. https://www.census.gov/library/publications/1971/demo/p60-80.html.

U.S. Census Bureau. *Per Capita Income, Median Family Money Income, and Low Income Status in 1969 for States, Standard Metropolitan Statistical Areas, and Counties: 1970.* June 1974. https://www2.census.gov/library/publications/decennial/1970/pc-s1-supplementary-reports/pc-s1-63.pdf.

Visram, Talib. *The deep-rooted myth of meritocracy is widening the racial wealth gap.* The Samuel DuBois Cook Center on Social Equity at Duke University. Accessed February 18, 2023. https://socialequity.duke.edu/news/the-deep-rooted-myth-of-meritocracy-is-widening-the-racial-wealth-gap/.

Waldroff, Kirk. *Healing the political divide: How did we become such a divided nation, and how can psychologists help us bridge the gap?* American Psychological Association. January 1, 2021 https://www.apa.org/monitor/2021/01/healing-political-divide.

Wenger, Jeffrey B., and Melanie A. Zaber. *Most Americans Consider Themselves Middle-Class. But Are They?* The RAND Corporation. May 14, 2021 https://www.rand.org/blog/2021/05/most-americans-consider-themselves-middle-class-but.html.

Wikipedia contributors. *Causes of Income Inequality in the United States.* Wikipedia, February 16, 2023. https://en.wikipedia.org/wiki/Causes_of_income_inequality_in_the_United_States.

Wikipedia contributors. *FCC Fairness Doctrine*. Wikipedia, January 26, 2023. https://en.wikipedia.org/wiki/Fairness_doctrine.

Wikipedia contributors. *Meritocracy*. Wikipedia, January 22, 2023. https://en.wikipedia.org/wiki/Meritocracy.

Williams, Trina R. *Asset-building Policy as a Response to Wealth Inequality: Drawing Implications from the Homestead Act.* Center for Social Development. https://openscholarship.wustl.edu/cgi/viewcontent.cgi?article=1106&context=csd_research.

Wolff, Edward. *Household Wealth Trends in the United States, 1962 to 2016: Has Middle Class Wealth Recovered?* National Bureau of Economic Research. December 4, 2017. https://www.nber.org/papers/w24085.

Women of Color Network, Inc. *We Empower Women of Color Activists & Advocates to Fight Violence against ALL Women.* Accessed February 18, 2023. https://wocninc.org/.

ABOUT THE AUTHOR

Richard E. Rawson, Psy.D. is an accomplished author and entrepreneur with a master's in business administration and a doctorate in clinical psychology. With extensive experience ghostwriting for well-known authors, operating a marketing agency, and providing behavioral health services, he developed a passion for social justice and equity that stems from his upbringing during the tumultuous era of the 1960s and 1970s and his growing awareness of the entrenched inequality that continually suppresses individuals and entire communities to this day. He wrote *Empowering Communities* to make a difference in the lives of those affected by unequal distribution of resources, opportunities, and power.